Case Law in Physical Education and School Sport:

A Guide to Good Practice

Peter Whitlam

baalpe

ISBN-13: 978-1-902523-77-6
ISBN-10: 1-902523-77-6

**British Association of Advisers and Lecturers
in Physical Education (baalpe)**
University College Worcester
Henwick Grove
Worcester
WR2 6AJ
Tel: 01905-855584
Fax: 01905-855594
Email: admin.baalpe@worc.ac.uk
Website: www.baalpe.org

Author
Peter Whitlam

Editor
Aislinn Kelly

Assistant Editor
Jennifer Smith

Designer
Leanne Taylor

Indexer
Glyn Sutcliffe

Published on behalf of baalpe by

Coachwise Business Solutions
Coachwise Ltd
Chelsea Close
Off Amberley Road
Armley
Leeds LS12 4HP
Tel: 0113-231 1310 Fax: 0113-231 9606
Email: enquiries@coachwisesolutions.co.uk
Website: www.coachwisesolutions.co.uk

040183

ACKNOWLEDGEMENTS

This book is dedicated to Deryck Williams, sometime President, General Secretary and Safety Officer for the British Association of Advisers and Lecturers in Physical Education (baalpe); former Chair of the baalpe Safety Committee; original author of *Safe Practice in Physical Education and School Sport*; independent expert witness and former local education authority adviser for physical education.

The author would also like to thank the following for their assistance with this book:

Sarah and Anne Whitlam for typing the manuscript; Deryck Williams, Geoff Kirkby, Norman Eve and Jan Roman for reading, amending and improving the script; Professor Robert Clark, former Dean of the School of Legal Studies, Wolverhampton University, for access to the Lexis database; Geoff Edmondson, Norman Eve, John Severs and Deryck Williams for providing transcripts to some of the unreported cases; Mick Flannigan and Zurich Municipal for information and summaries of some of the cases contained in the book; Informa Professional Publications for information relating to the Woodroffe-Hedley case in Sports Law Administration and Practice; Kathryn Hume, Wragge and Company, for a summary of the Darby case; Keith Spencer for helping to provide information relating to the Drew case; The O-Pro Group for details of the *G (a child) versus Lancashire County Council* case in *No Mouthguard No Defence* 2001.

BIOGRAPHY OF THE AUTHOR

Peter Whitlam holds higher degrees in law and physical education. He has substantial experience of teaching physical education in the primary, secondary and higher education sectors. He was a senior inspector with a local education authority before becoming General Secretary to the British Association of Advisers and Lecturers in Physical Education (baalpe) and an independent consultant. He is currently the project manager for health and safety with baalpe. He is a co-author of *Safe Practice in Physical Education and School Sport* (baalpe, 2004)[1] and has contributed to publications on risk assessment in physical education and school sport. He also tutors a university course on Sports Law at Oxford Brookes. He was a member of the NOF Committee for Physical Education and School Sport and the QCA Steering Committee for the National Project in Physical Education. Peter is a trained legal expert witness and an Ofsted inspector.

[1] British Association of Advisers and Lecturers in Physical Education (baalpe) (2004) *Safe Practice in Physical Education and School Sport.* Leeds: Coachwise Solutions. ISBN: 1 902523 68 7.

CONTENTS   PAGE

TABLE OF STATUTES

Case Law in Physical Education and School Sport:
A Guide to Good Practice

Introduction to Case Law in Physical Education and School Sport

TABLE OF CASES

Chapter 2 comprises an overview of risk management in physical education and school sport. Chapter 5 contains the case law relevant to good practice.

CHAPTER 2

CASE	YEAR	LAW REPORT REFERENCE	PAGE
Bolton v Stone	1951	AC 850 (and Chapter 5, Case 38)	23, 124
Condon v Basi	1985	2 All ER 453 (and Chapter 5, Case 22)	23, 100
Jones v Manchester Corporation	1958	2 QB 852	25
Letang v Cooper	1965	1 QB 232	23
Lewis v Brookshaw	1970	120 NLJ 413	22
Lyes v Middlesex County Council	1962	61 LGR 443	24
Marshall v Bolton	1999	Unreported	47
Nydegger v Don Boscoe Preparatory High School	1985	Canada	32
R v Brown	1993	2 All ER 75	31
R v Moore	1898	14 TLR 229	31
Stokes v Guest, Kean and Nettleford (Bolts and Nuts) Ltd	1968	1 WLR 1776	24
Williams v Eady	1893	10 TLR 41	23
Wilsher v East Sussex Health Authority	1986	QB 730	24

CHAPTER 5

5.1 Cases of Negligence Relating to People: School Staff, Coaches and Volunteers

CASE	ACTIVITY	PHASE	TITLE	YEAR	COURT	SOURCE	PAGE
1	Asthma	Secondary	Hipployte v Bexley London Borough	1994	CA	Lexis	65
2	Athletics	Secondary	Porter v LB of Barking and Dagenham	1990	HC	Lexis	67
3	Cricket	Secondary	Barfoot v East Sussex County Council	1939	Cty Ct	Croner	69
4	Field studies	Secondary	Porter v City of Bradford M C	1985	CA	Lexis	70
5	Gymnastics	Primary	Felgate v Middlesex County Council	1954	Cty Ct	Croner	72
6	Gymnastics	Primary	Mills v Staffordshire County Council	2002	Cty Ct	Unreported	73
7	Gymnastics	Secondary	Gibbs v Barking Corporation	1936	CA	Lexis	75
8	Horse riding	Adult	Starling v Hoogeman	1983	HC	Lexis	76
9	Play	Pre-school	Burton v Canto Play Group	1989	HC	Lexis	77
10	Play	Primary	Dean v Municipal Mutual Assurance Ltd	1981	CA	Lexis	79
11	Rock climbing	Adult	Graham v Newcastle City Council	2000	Cty Ct	Zurich	81
12	Rugby	Secondary	Affutu-Nartay v Clark	1994	CB	Lexis	82
13	Rugby	Secondary	Smolden v Whitworth	1996	CA	Lexis	84
14	Rugby	Adult	Vowles v Evans	2003	HC	*Daily Mail*	86
15	Scuba diving	Adult	Percival v Corporation of Leicester	1962	HC	Lexis	87
16	Self-defence	Adult	Harrington v South Glamorgan Health Authority	1996	Cty Ct	Unreported	89
17	Swimming	Primary	Burke v Cardiff City Council	1986	CA	Lexis	91

Swimming	Primary	Jones v Cheshire County Council	1997	Cty Ct	Unreported	93
Swimming	Secondary	Clarke v Bethnal Green Borough Council	1939	HC	Lexis	95
Trampolining	Adult	Stenner v Taff-Ely Borough Council	1987	CA	Lexis	96

5.2 Cases of Negligence Relating to People: Pupils and Participants

CASE	ACTIVITY	PHASE	TITLE	YEAR	COURT	SOURCE	PAGE
21	Athletics	Adult	Morrell v Owen	1993	HC	Lexis	98
22	Football	Adult	Condon v Basi	1985	CA	Lexis	100
23	Football	Adult	Perry v McGuckin	1990	HC	Lexis	101
24	Football	Adult	Elliott v Saunders	1994	HC	Lexis	103
25	Football	Adult	McCord v Swansea Football Club	1997	HC	Lexis	105
26	Football	Adult	Watson v Gray	1999	CA	Lexis	107
27	Golf	Secondary	Cuthbertson v Merchiston Castle School	2000	Sh Ct	Zurich	108
28	Golf	Adult	Brewer v Delo	1967	HC	Lexis	109
29	Gymnastics	Secondary	Wright v Cheshire County Council	1952	CA	Lexis	110
30	Gymnastics	Adult	Steward v Curry	1995	CA	Lexis	112
31	Horse riding	Adult	Wooldridge v Sumner	1962	CA	Lexis	113
32	Play	Pre-school	Dyer v Ilfracombe Urban District Council	1955	CA	Lexis	115
33	Rock climbing	Adult	Young v Taunton Dean Borough Council	2000	Cty Ct	Zurich	116
34	Rowing	Secondary	Thelma (owners) v University College School	1953	Cty Ct	Lexis	117

5.3 Cases of Negligence Relating to Context: Facilities

CASE	ACTIVITY	PHASE	TITLE	YEAR	COURT	SOURCE	PAGE
35	Athletics	Secondary	Futcher v Hertfordshire LEA	1997	Cty Ct	Unreported	119
36	Athletics	Adult	Comer v Govs of St Patrick's RC Primary School	1997	CA	Lexis	120
37	Badminton	Secondary	Peacey v Havering LEA	1999	Cty Ct	Zurich	122
38	Cricket	Adult	Bolton v Stone	1951	HL	Lexis	124
39	Cricket	Adult	Miller v Jackson	1977	CA	Lexis	126
40	Cricket	Adult	Douch v Reading Borough Council	2001	Cty Ct	Zurich	128
41	Football	Adult	Jones v Northampton Borough Council	1990	CA	Lexis	129
42	Games	Secondary	Ralph v London City Council	1947	HC	Lexis	131
43	Games	Adult	Gilmore v London City Council	1938	HC	Lexis	132
44	Games	Adult	Mutimer v Margate Corporation	1956	HC	Lexis	134
45	Games	Adult	Taylor v Corby Borough Council	2000	Cty Ct	Zurich	135
46	General	Adult	Goncalves v Bournemouth Borough Council	2001	Cty Ct	Zurich	136
47	Ice hockey	Primary	Murray v Harringay Arena	1951	CA	Lexis	138
48	Play	Primary	Ellis v Fulham Borough Council	1937	HC	Lexis	139
49	Play	Primary	Sutton v Bootle Corporation	1946	CA	Lexis	141
50	Play	Primary	Bates v Stone Parish Council	1954	CA	Lexis	142
51	Play	Primary	Morgan v Blunden	1986	CA	Lexis	143
52	Residential	Secondary	Dickinson v Cornwall County Council	2000	Cty Ct	Zurich	145
53	Rugby	Primary	Steed v Cheltenham Borough Council	2000	Cty Ct	Zurich	147
54	Rugby	Adult	Simms v Leigh Rugby Football Club	1968	HC	Lexis	148
55	Skiing	Adult	Owen v Rossendale Borough Council	2001	Cty Ct	Zurich	150

CASE	ACTIVITY	PHASE	TITLE	YEAR	COURT	SOURCE	PAGE
56	Swimming	Secondary	Simmons v Borough of Huntingdon	1936	HC	Lexis	151
57	Swimming	Adult	Parkowski v City of Wellington Corporation	1958	Privy C	Lexis	152
58	Swimming	Adult	Davies v Borough of Tenby	1974	CA	Lexis	154
59	Swimming	Adult	McEwan v Edensis Saunasium	1986	CA	Lexis	156
60	Swimming	Adult	Bains v York City Council	1992	CA	Lexis	158
61	Swimming	Adult	O'Shea v RB of Kingston upon Thames	1994	CA	Lexis	160
62	Swimming	Adult	Ratcliff v McConnell	1998	CA	Lexis	162
63	Swimming	Adult	Tomlinson v Congleton District Council	2001	CA	Zurich	164

5.4 Cases of Negligence Relating to Context: Equipment

CASE	ACTIVITY	PHASE	TITLE	YEAR	COURT	SOURCE	PAGE
64	Cricket	Secondary	Lott v Devon County Council	2001	Cty Ct	Zurich	166
65	Gymnastics	Primary	Butler v Cheshire County Council	1996	Cty Ct	Unreported	167
66	Gymnastics	Primary	Peel v Ashfield Gymnastics Club	2001	Cty Ct	Unreported	169
67	Gymnastics	Secondary	Beaumont v Surrey County Council	1968	HC	Lexis	171
68	Gymnastics	Secondary	Tapping v Kent County Council	1990	HC	Lexis	173
69	Gymnastics	Adult	Fowles v Bedfordshire County Council	1995	CA	Lexis	175
70	Hockey	Secondary	Cassidy v City of Manchester	1995	CA	Lexis	177
71	Outdoor adventure	Secondary	Ramsay v Kings School	1999	Cty Ct	Unreported	179
72	Play	Pre-school	Coates v Rawtenstall Borough Council	1957	HC	Lexis	181
73	Play	Pre-school	Chapman v Rhondda-Cynon-Taff Borough Council	2001	Cty Ct	Zurich	183

5.5 Cases of Negligence Relating to Activity Organisation: Preparation

CASE	ACTIVITY	PHASE	PAGE	YEAR	COURT	SOURCE	PAGE
74	Assault courses	Secondary	Morgan v Avonhurst School	1995	CA	Lexis	185
75	Climbing	Adult	Pope v Cuthbertson	1995	HC	Lexis	187
76	Climbing	Adult	Woodroffe-Hedley v Cuthbertson	1997	HC	Informa	189
77	Dance	Adult	Hill v Durham County Council	2000	CA	Zurich	191
78	Gymnastics	Secondary	A (a minor) v Leeds City Council	1999	Cty Ct	Zurich	192
79	Gymnastics	Secondary	Cooke v Kent County Council	1949	HC	Lexis	193
80	Gymnastics	Secondary	Moore v Hampshire County Council	1981	CA	Lexis	195

5.6 Cases of Negligence Relating to Activity Organisation: Teaching and Organisation

CASE	ACTIVITY	PHASE	TITLE	YEAR	COURT	SOURCE	PAGE
81	Athletics	Secondary	Darby (a minor) v Worcestershire County Council	2003	Cty Ct	Wragge	197
82	Gaelic football	Secondary	Ward v Donegal Vocation Education Committee	1994	Ireland	Zurich	198
83	Golf	Adult	Horton v Jackson	1996	CA	Lexis	199
84	Gymnastics	Primary	Cotton v Kent County Council	1983	HC	Lexis	201
85	Gymnastics	Primary	Jones v Hampshire County Council	1997	CA	Lexis	203
86	Gymnastics	Secondary	Heffer v Wiltshire County Council	1996	HC	Unreported	205
87	Gymnastics	Secondary	Povey v Governors of Rydal School	1969	HC	Lexis	207
88	Gymnastics	Secondary	Gleave v Lancashire County Council	1951		Croner	209
89	Gymnastics	Secondary	Kershaw v Hampshire County Council	1982		Croner	210
90	Gymnastics	Secondary	Ogden v Rotherham MBC	1997	Cty Ct	Unreported	211
91	Hockey	Secondary	G (a child) v Lancashire County Council	2000	Cty Ct	O-Pro	212
92	Physical education	Primary	R v Chair and Govs Cwnfelinfach Primary School	2001	HC	Unreported	214
93	Rugby	Secondary	van Oppen v Bedford Charity Trustees	1988	HC	Lexis	216
94	Skiing	Secondary	C (a child) v W School	2002	CA	Croner	218
95	Sports day	Primary	Simmonds v Isle of Wight Council	2003	HC	Daily Mail	220
96	Tennis	Primary	Bell v Staffordshire County Council	2003	Cty Ct	Zurich	222
97	Trampolining	Primary	Villella v North Bedfordshire Borough Council	1983	HC	Lexis	224
98	Trampolining	Secondary	Kenyon v Lancashire County Council	2001	Cty Ct	Unreported	226
99	Trampolining	Secondary	Stapley v Ashford Borough Council	1989	HC	Lexis	227

5.7 Cases Relating to Health and Safety

CASE	ACTIVITY	PHASE	TITLE	YEAR	COURT	SOURCE	PAGE
100	Adventure	Secondary	R v Ellis	2003	Cn Ct	*Daily Mail*	229
101	Adventure	Pre-school	Moulem v City of Carlisle	1994	HC	Lexis	231
102	Canoeing	Secondary	R v Kite	1996	CA	Lexis	233
103	Horse riding	Secondary	Leeds City Council v Phoenix Equestrian Centre	2003	HC	*Daily Mail*	235
104	Swimming	Secondary	A silent drowning case	1995	HC	NAHT	237

5.8 Cases Relating to the Offences Against the Person Act 1981: Violence in Sport

CASE	ACTIVITY	PHASE	TITLE	YEAR	COURT	SOURCE	PAGE
105	Football	Adult	R v Birkin	1988	CA	Lexis	239
106	Football	Adult	R v Shervill	1989	CA	Lexis	240
107	Football	Adult	R v Lincoln	1990	CA	Lexis	241
108	Football	Adult	R v Rogers	1993	CA	Lexis	242
109	Rugby	Secondary	R v Calton	1998	CA	*Daily Telegraph*	243
110	Rugby	Adult	R v Goodwin	1995	CA	Lexis	245
111	Rugby	Adult	R v Lloyd	1989	CA	Lexis	247

5.9 Cases Relating to Child Abuse in Sport

CASE	ACTIVITY	PHASE	TITLE	YEAR	COURT	SOURCE	PAGE
112	Swimming	Secondary	R v Drew	2001	Cn Ct	The Times	248

KEY

CA	Court of Appeal
Cn Ct	Crown Court
Cty Ct	County Court
HC	High Court
HL	House of Lords
Privy C	Privy Council
Sh Ct	Sheriff's Court (Scotland)

Case Law in Physical Education and School Sport:
A Guide to Good Practice

Chapter 1
Introduction to Case Law in Physical Education and School Sport

1.0 INTRODUCTION

This textbook has been written by a teacher for teachers, coaches and other adults working in schools or related *provider* contexts. Any errors of fact or interpretation are the responsibility of the author.

The purpose of this book is not to interpret the finer points of law. In fact, it is to identify and reinforce the principles of good practice and standards of care in physical education and school sport, based on decisions made by the courts. The over-riding principle is not to tell the adults responsible what they *must* do, but to inform them of what they need to *be aware of* when teaching in this environment.

Sources of case information are provided where they have been easily obtained. Cases that are relevant to good practice principles are included, whether or not all the case details have been sourced. A selection of reported case law that is relevant to physical education and school sport, together with a selection of unreported cases, is used to provide guidance on good practice. Selection has been limited to issues relating to safe management of the subject. Some cases involving adults are included because of their relevance to the school context. Summarising the available judgments produces a helpful and broad range of implications, from which a system of good practice can be extrapolated – a system that identifies the foreseeable generic and activity-specific safety principles.

In addition to providing guidance on foreseeable risks, case analysis highlights the importance of:

- competence when teaching or coaching activities
- appropriate supervision
- involving pupils in their own safety in a manner appropriate to their age, experience and ability
- safe working environments and secure equipment
- systematic preparation for activities
- following regular and approved practice
- playing within the rules and spirit of games.

1.1 HOW SHOULD THIS BOOK BE USED?

Teachers, coaches and other adults working in schools or related *provider* contexts can use this book in the following ways:

- Adopt the practice recommended in Chapter 2 of having safety and accident or *near miss* analysis as a regular, brief agenda item in meetings.

- Base their risk assessments on the triangle format described in Chapter 2.

- Compare their documentation with the *good practice* summary in Chapter 4 and determine whether they have anything to learn.

- Select cases from Chapter 5 for discussion in team meetings.

- Select cases, delete the *issues* and create their own *good practice* issues through discussion.

- Collate phase cases (eg primary or secondary) or activity cases, identify any patterns of cause in the incidents and determine *good practice* from these.

- Compare similar cases in order to identify differences in fact and, therefore, in outcome.

- Consider the judgments that surprise them and analyse whether these have any impact on their own practice.

- Compare their school/department accident report analyses with the cases and determine whether they have anything to learn.

- Consider whether the discussed incidents could happen to them. Determine whether their documented procedures and routines are sufficiently clear and detailed, and whether they are consistently applied to avoid such incidents. Compare their procedures and routines with the case issues.

- Select case summaries for use with specific members of their team as part of the team's individual professional development, in order to make the team members more aware of the consequences of their actions.

- Track changes in judgments over time in order to identify trends and determine whether there are any implications for them.

Chapter Two
Risk Management in Physical Education and School Sport

2.0 THE RISK CONTINUUM

Totally safe or risk-free situations do not occur in physical education and school sport because they are practical activities involving movement, often at speed and in confined areas shared with others. The *risk continuum* (Figure 1) identifies the acceptable range of risk within which school staff and other adults make decisions every day. Occasionally, there have been serious injuries and tragedies where the level of risk involved has gone beyond this acceptable range, reaching much higher levels of risk or danger. This is when harm is likely to occur. These high-risk situations usually arise when the level of forethought, anticipation or planning by the adult responsible has been inadequate.

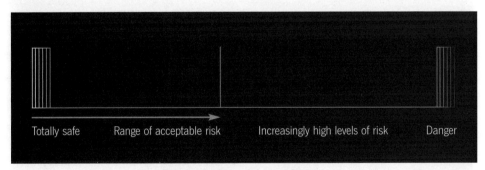

Figure 1: The risk continuum

Physical education and school sport involve providing young people with appropriate challenges within acceptable levels of risk. Individual school staff and employers, through policy and practice, decide to set and accept varying levels of risk according to the circumstances of particular teaching situations. School staff, contracted coaches and volunteers make daily decisions within the acceptable range of risk. They are good at doing this. Concerns about working with high levels of risk are often unfounded because the obvious concern then limits the teacher's (or other adult's) willingness to continue. The task is altered to reduce the risk and work then continues within the acceptable range. Serious situations only arise when the member of staff, coach or volunteer fails to use observation and analysis to recognise that the activity has moved into the high-risk danger area.

It is good practice to discuss regularly, as a staff or department, any injury situations or *near misses* that have occurred in physical education and school sport. A regular item on meeting agendas will provide a brief opportunity to review current practice in relation to any accidents, incidents or emerging patterns of cause of injury. This routine enables those involved in teaching the subject to reflect beyond the immediate, apparent cause of any injuries, identify the organisational causes and consider whether the subject procedures, routines and documentation should have prevented the injuries occurring. From this, it can be determined whether the documentation requires further development, or whether a particular adult would benefit from some relevant professional development or support. Those applying this practice have recognised that incidents involving injury are reduced.

Developing the habit of considering risk management in a structured way helps schools to address safety issues thoroughly and to a suitable and sufficient standard. This is often described as *reasonable forethought*. One such format, designed by members of the Safety Committee of the British Association of Advisers and Lecturers in Physical Education (baalpe), is set out in Figure 2.

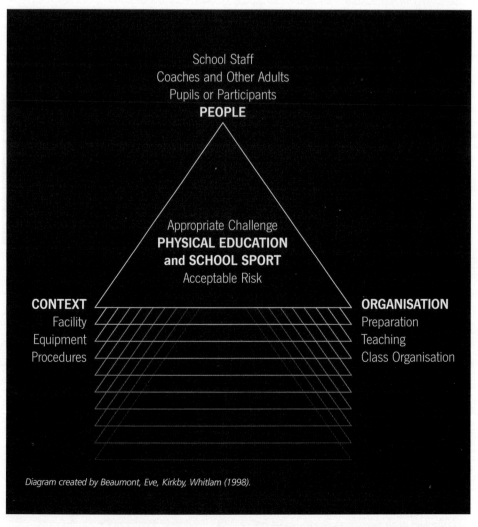

Diagram created by Beaumont, Eve, Kirkby, Whitlam (1998).

Figure 2: Safe practice in physical education

2.1 FACTORS INFLUENCING THE LEVEL OF RISK

The following three factors influence the level of risk in physical education and school sport:

Factor 1: Issues relating to the *people* involved in the session

School staff and other adults:

- have a duty of care for those they are working with (ie a responsibility for their safety)

- have three basic legal duties:
  - to know and to follow the employer's policy and guidelines for health and safety
  - to pass on information regarding any health and safety concerns to their line manager
  - to do whatever is within their power to prevent further harm arising from the reported concern

- need particular competences to be responsible for groups:
  - expertise (qualifications/experience/competence) across the range of activities they teach in terms of technical knowledge about the activities, progressive practices, safety and knowledge of rules in order to referee stringently
  - observation and analysis skills in order to identify anything that is potentially unsafe and respond to it
  - class management/organisation/control in order to immediately stop an activity if it is deemed to be potentially hazardous

- need to have sufficient knowledge of the pupils' medical and individual needs.

Pupils should:

- be involved in their own safety

- develop competence in movement, techniques, skills, tactics and choreography

- be confident in their movement activities

- behave appropriately so as not to create risk situations

- be appropriately supervised as they undertake leadership roles or progress towards more independent activities.

Factor 2: Issues relating to the *context* in which the activity takes place

Facilities should:

- provide hazard-free work surfaces
- be of a sufficient size to meet the demands of the activity
- be regularly maintained
- be used appropriately.

Equipment should be:

- of an appropriate size to suit the age and ability of the individual
- regularly maintained
- inspected annually
- regularly checked for wear and tear
- checked before use
- stored safely
- disposed of effectively when condemned
- used for the purpose it was designed.

Procedures need to address:

- safe practice
- risk assessment
- regular and approved practice
- accidents and emergencies
- portfolios of records such as medical, individual needs, assessment and attendance
- the process of informing pupils and parents of essential organisation issues.

Factor 3: Issues relating to the *organisation* of the activity

Preparation involves:

- detailed and differentiated schemes of work

- a clear lesson structure

- adequate warm-up based on safe exercise principles

- a knowledge of the pupils, including their performance potential.

Teaching, class management and organisation should ensure that:

- tasks match pupil capability

- methodology is appropriate to the risk issues within the activity

- progressive practices enable improvement to occur

- pupils are involved in the learning of these progressive practices

- pupils are matched according to size, experience, ability and confidence

- regular and approved practice is followed.

The summary of good practice principles in Chapter 4 and the organisation of the case law used in Chapter 5 follow this model.

It is perfectly acceptable for other risk assessment models to be preferred. Whichever model is used, it is important that schools are able to demonstrate that they can manage accidents and emergencies in an efficient manner.

2.2 THE REALITY

Physical education and school sport are exciting areas of activity to teach and experience. There is increasingly hard evidence of the benefits of participation in these areas. The slight possibility of someone being hurt, or the rare instance of an allegation that the teacher has not matched expected professional standards, should not deter anyone from teaching or participating in the context of appropriate challenge and acceptable risk. When reading the case law summarised in this book, responsible adults should remember that addressing what is deemed to be good practice is the positive outcome.

They should also keep the frequency of injury in physical education and school sport in perspective. It is important to be aware that there are nearly 1500 million pupil-days in each academic year in the UK. Within this huge number, the Health and Safety Executive annual reports indicate that, typically, between three and six individuals die, and some 5000 suffer a major injury, in education as a whole. A major injury is a situation requiring at least three days off school or a visit to a hospital for any reason and for any length of time. For each one of these 5000 major injuries, there are a further 10 injuries requiring first aid and about 400 very minor injuries or *near misses*. This is a relatively small total compared with the number of pupil-days in an academic year. Within these figures for education, injuries arising from physical education and school sport comprise a fraction of the statistics. Injuries in physical education are relatively rare. School staff are good at what they do and they should remember this.

Chapter Three
An Outline of the Law

3.0 THE CONTEXT

School staff, contracted coaches and volunteers operate within a complex legal framework. Figure 3 provides a simplified explanation of the elements of law considered in this book. The relevant elements of the legal system include civil and criminal law, with an emphasis on negligence, health and safety, violent conduct in sport and child abuse.

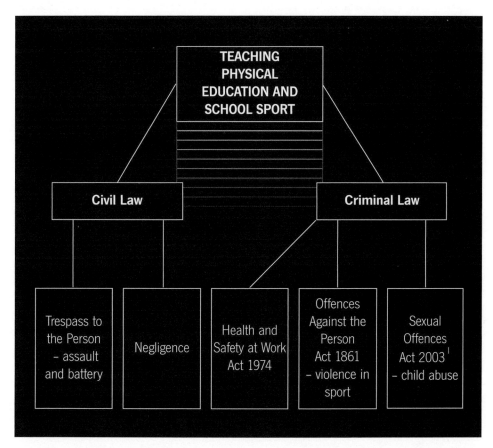

Figure 3: Aspects of the legal system relevant to the teaching of physical education and school sport

English and Welsh Law are common. The legal systems in Scotland and Northern Ireland are distinct in some ways from those in England and Wales, but the principles of good practice are the same.

A comparison of civil and criminal law terminology is given in Figure 4 on page 28.

---

[1] Prior to this Act, cases relating to child abuse were pursued under a range of statute such as the Rape Act 1971 or, if appropriate, the Offences Against the Person Act 1861.

3.1 CIVIL LAW

Civil law evolves over time as individuals resort to the courts because of harm or damage resulting from acts of omission or commission by other people. In physical education and school sport, damage is usually in the form of injury. The claimant sues the other person (the defendant) for damages in the form of compensation. If the action is successful, the defendant is found liable (ie responsible). Where damages are awarded as a result of a successful action, they are assessed on the basis that they are to compensate the claimant rather than to punish the defendant. In a civil case, the level of necessary proof is based on a balance of probability (likely) which is lower than in criminal cases where the required level is beyond reasonable doubt (sure).

Litigation in physical education and school sport has increased over the years. Solicitors may now advertise for work – the slogan *No Win, No Fee* seen in the media attracts custom. Young people and their parents have become more aware of their legal rights and, consequently, are prepared to seek compensation through civil action. Also, irregularities are more easily exposed through crises such as the Lyme Bay canoeing tragedy (see Case 102, page 233) and increasingly numerous written regulations. Unless personal accident insurance is taken out, which normally covers injury with permanent effects, the only compensation available to an injured person is through a civil court claim for damages.

Recent media coverage of cases has indicated that the judiciary is applying a common-sense approach to scurrilous litigation. In some instances, initial judgments in favour of claimants have been reversed and claimants have been required to repay any compensation that they have received and pay court costs. This approach will help to maintain a sensible approach to initiating litigation in search of compensation.

3.1.1 Types of civil action

There are three levels of fault recognised in law:

- Intention – when the infliction of an injury is planned.

- Recklessness – when the inflictor realises that the act may result in injury, but does not care.

- Carelessness – when the infliction of an injury is considered to be unintentional.

Compensation for injury caused by participants in physical education and school sport may be obtained through one of two ways. The first, but least common, is that of assault and battery, which is technically referred to as *trespass to the person*. In *Lewis v Brookshaw 1970* (*120 NLJ 413*), civil damages for assault arising from deliberate or reckless foul play (see *Intention* and *Recklessness* above) outside the laws of the game, were awarded for a broken leg in a football match.

The second and most common offence is that of negligence. The difference between trespass and negligence is identified by Lord Denning in *Letang v Cooper 1965* (*1QB 232*) as the intentional offer of force or violence to another (see *Intention* and *Recklessness* above). Without the evidence of intention or recklessness, the only course of action is negligence, where injury arises from an unintentional action or omission (see *Carelessness* above). The majority of cases seeking compensation in the civil courts is based on alleged negligence. This is because it is easier to obtain a successful outcome by not needing to prove that the cause of the injury was intentional. Cases, such as *Condon v Basi 1985* (*2 All ER 453*), have been initiated on allegations both of trespass, requiring a need to prove an intention to cause injury, and negligence, with the case decided ultimately on the issue of negligence.

3.2 NEGLIGENCE

The issue of negligence may arise when an individual fails to maintain the standard of care expected in the particular circumstances to protect others from the unreasonable risk of harm. An allegation of negligence requires the following four factors:

- a duty of care to the other person (ie having some responsibility for them)

- breaching that duty (ie being careless)

- damage arising from the breach (ie injury due to the carelessness)

- foreseeability (ie that the exposure to the harm was unreasonable and fell below the expected level of care).

If all four factors are present, negligence may be proven. The adults involved may have been careless, but only a judge in a court of law can determine that someone was actually negligent, by finding them liable for the injury sustained. This decision is based on the specific circumstances of the claim.

Inevitably, injuries will occur in physical education and school sport because of their active nature. It is the element of foreseeability that may impose a liability of negligence. Judges apply what is called the *but for* test, meaning that the injury would not have occurred *but for* the action of the person being held responsible (ie the defendant in a court case). Reasonable foresight is illustrated in *Bolton v Stone 1951* (*AC 850*). In this case, it is set at the level of guarding against the probable, rather than simply possible, consequences of a failure to take care.

3.2.1 Standard of care

The standard of care expected of a teacher is set out in *Williams v Eady 1893 10* (*TLR 41*), where it is described as that of a careful parent. This standard has, however, been modified and updated in *Lyes v Middlesex County Council 1962* (*61 LGR 443*), in which it is judged that the application of the careful parent test should be in the context of the school rather than the home, because a teacher clearly has responsibility for more children at any one time and in a different environment from the home. While the careful parent analogy is no longer accurate, it still reminds those in schools of their responsibility for the welfare, safety and education of children in their care. Modernisation of the school workforce has broadened the scope of this level of professional responsibility to include all employees of the school, paid coaches who may be contracted to provide particular services, and unpaid volunteers contributing to physical education and school sport programmes.

The standard of care has been set at that of a reasonably competent person working at an acceptable level of expertise and in the same area of activity. Lord Justice Glidewell in *Wilsher v Essex Health Authority 1986* (*QB 730*) identified a claim of inexperience as a possible loophole defence against a charge of negligence. He closed this by determining that an inexperienced member of staff, coach or volunteer would be judged at the same standard as more experienced colleagues to avoid inexperience being frequently used as a defence.

A review of case law with regard to duty of care indicates that a realistic view of responsibility is usually taken. Perfection is not expected, but a standard appropriate to a competent professional person is required.

The concept of *in loco parentis* (in the place of a parent) is no longer applied because the responsibilities of teachers are no longer compared to those of parents. Also, with the evolving modernisation of the school workforce, all school staff, those contracted to provide services and volunteers have a duty of care to the pupils for whom they are responsible. There is no distinction in the standard of care expected between teachers or others working with pupils, other than that set by the level of expertise the individual offers. Thus, the principles identified in the cases apply to all who work with pupils, regardless of their status or title.

3.2.2 A higher duty of care

In *Stokes v Guest, Keen and Nettleford* (*Bolts and Nuts*) *Limited 1968* (*1 WLR 1776*) it was determined that, when defendants have a level of knowledge and experience that is higher than expected of a reasonable person acting in their position or capacity, they are judged by that enhanced standard of foresight. This defines a higher duty of care, in that adults with specialist expertise or qualifications are expected to have a greater insight into, and awareness of, the consequences of their actions. Thus, *specialists* in a particular area, or adults leading higher risk activities, are deemed to have a higher duty of care (ie a higher level of responsibility) for those in their care.

3.2.3 Defences against a charge of negligence

Significant levels of protection exist against allegations of negligence. These are:

3.2.3.1 Vicarious liability

Employers are responsible for the acts of their employees when they are acting in the proper course of their employment. This strict liability would apply to anything undertaken as part of any contractual or sanctioned voluntary duty. For this reason, those working in physical education and school sport are expected to work within guidelines and policies laid down by their employers, to gain permission for particular activities, to follow regular and approved practice, and to maintain an up-to-date awareness of the subject through continuing professional development.

Where staff are not qualified or competent, but have been placed in a situation by their employers or the employers' representative such as a head teacher, employers may be directly liable for negligence, as established in *Jones v Manchester Corporation 1958* (*2 QB 852*).

3.2.3.2 Contributory negligence

The Law Reform (Contributory Negligence) Act 1945 established that liability, or responsibility for injuries, may be apportioned by the court. Claimants' acts or omissions that contribute to their injuries may be taken into account when compensation is determined. The level of compensation may then be reduced according to each claimant's percentage of responsibility for contributing to the injury. The younger the person injured, the less likely they are to be considered to have an awareness of their contribution to the situation. A similar decision is likely to be made for those with some form of learning difficulty.

3.2.3.3 Voluntary assumption of risk

This principle allows courts to refuse compensation to claimants. It is based on the premise that participants knowingly accept the possibility of injury when taking part in activities within the laws and spirit of the particular activity. It does not allow for the infliction of harm outside the laws and spirit of a game, therefore intentional or reckless infliction of injury cannot be defended under this principle. It is a concept that would apply to adult participation in sport. It may also apply to voluntary participation by young people, but only in very specific circumstances.

It would be difficult to apply this defence to pupils in physical education lessons that require participation as part of the National Curriculum. It would also be difficult to show that young people, particularly, were fully cognisant of the risks involved and were legally competent to accept them.

The only consent to injury that parents have to accept on behalf of their children is that which arises as the result of an accident, the consequences of which would be unforeseeable.

3.2.3.4 Consent by the participant

This is very similar to a voluntary assumption of risk. It is a defence used only in trespass cases, such as in martial arts or contact sports, where physical contact forms the basis of the activity. Consent to injury is implied from participation in the activity, but only to the degree of force normally expected and, again, within the rules and spirit of the sport.

3.2.4 Good practice defences against allegations of negligence

Adhering to the following guidelines could help in the case of an allegation of negligence.

3.2.4.1 A portfolio of records

Evidence of collating and using the following can be of great value when refuting allegations of negligence:

- policies and guidelines

- schemes of work

- registers of attendance

- assessment records

- medical information

- risk assessments

- accident logs and analysis of these

- equipment maintenance reports

- minutes of meetings.

3.2.4.2 Regular and approved practice

Practice that is typical of that seen nationally rather than locally is deemed to be widely used because it is sound. Such practice is typical of that evident in local education authority schemes of work and national governing body or national association guidelines.

A related principle is that of using equipment only for the purpose it was designed. Improvisation of equipment or teaching situations should proceed only with very careful forethought in order to avoid the possibility of injury arising from makeshift arrangements.

3.2.4.3 Progression

Progressive practices enable young people to develop competence and confidence over time in more complex movement and skill application.

3.2.4.4 Comparable size, ability, experience and confidence

Matching these considerations when young people are weight-bearing, or when physical contact or an accelerating projectile (eg a cricket ball) form part of a teaching situation, provides a context in which young people may practise and improve safely.

3.2.4.5 Strict officiating

Knowing and applying the rules of a game stringently provides a safe and consistent context in which pupils may learn.

3.2.4.6 The adult's role in playing games

Adults should avoid playing a full part as a participant in a game with young people, due to the differences in strength and experience between adults and children. It is good practice to take a limited role in games, in order to set up situations that enable the pupils to learn from that participation. This would exclude involvement such as tackling, shooting with power and bowling or pitching with pace.

3.2.4.7 Codes of conduct

Codes of conduct that outline the expectations placed on participants are becoming more common. A code of conduct is a useful document, which helps to clarify the standards expected of those taking part, for the benefit of participants and parents. In extreme circumstances, it could be used as the basis for the early return of an individual from an event such as an adventure holiday, if the behaviour of the participant warrants this and the parents are aware of this as a condition of taking part.

It is a common misconception that consent forms signed by parents indemnify teachers from any claim for negligence. This is not so. Such disclaimers have no standing in law. The courts would not recognise this as absolving teachers of their responsibility before events take place. Under the principles of the Unfair Contract Terms Act 1977, minors have three further years after reaching the age of consent (18 years old) to retrospectively file a claim in their own right for injuries received as minors. This clearly sets a parental consent form as a participation agreement only. Such agreements do not absolve teachers from responsibility. They are simply signed statements indicating that parents have been informed, understand the risks involved in the activities and agree to comply with the conditions.

3.2.5 Statute within civil law

Judicial decisions and the issue of custom and practice constitute the main bases for claims of civil wrong. Very few acts of Parliament are relevant to civil claims. Exceptions to this include the Law Reform (Contributory Negligence) Act 1945 and the Occupiers' Liability Acts of 1957 and 1984, which are only used in civil contexts.

The Occupiers' Liability Act 1957 introduced a common duty of care for all lawful visitors to a site or facility. The occupier is required to take reasonable precautions to ensure that visitors are reasonably safe when using the premises for the intended purpose. The 1984 Act introduced a duty of care to trespassers where the occupier is aware of any risks on the premises to which some form of protection could reasonably be provided. A civil claim could be made if an occupier is shown to have, or is expected to have, an awareness of some defect on the premises that could lead to injury. The standard expected relates to that of negligence and includes awareness that children are likely to be less careful than adults – an obvious implication for school and leisure facilities.

PRINCIPLE	CIVIL CASES	CRIMINAL CASES
Unacceptable act against:	Individual	Society
Based on:	Common law evolving over time and arising from judgments and common rights	Statute
Proceedings:	Action or claim	Prosecution
Brought by:	Claimant	Criminal Prosecution Service, local authorities, Health and Safety Executive (HSE), Inland Revenue, Customs and Excise, etc
Defended by:	Defendant	Defendant
Verdict:	Liable or not liable	Guilty or acquitted
Objective:	Compensation	Punishment
Penalties:	Damages	Conviction leading to imprisonment, fine, probation or prohibition
Penalty paid to:	Claimant	State
Standard of proof:	Balance of probability (likely)	Beyond reasonable doubt (sure)

Figure 4: Understanding civil and criminal law differences

3.3 CRIMINAL LAW

Criminal law addresses offences that are serious enough to be deemed to be against society, rather than an individual. A successful prosecution requires a level of proof beyond reasonable doubt (sure – ie higher than that of civil cases). A guilty verdict results in a conviction against the state, with the penalty consisting of imprisonment, a fine, prohibition or probation. The punishment provides no direct benefit to the victim.

3.4 HEALTH AND SAFETY

Schools have been fully included in health and safety legislation since the enactment of the Health and Safety at Work Act 1974. This Act moved the emphasis from compensation to pro-active prevention of injury. The Act seeks to secure the health, safety and welfare of those at work and to protect others visiting and using the premises against risks to their health and safety that arise from the activities of those at work. By law, employers are responsible for health and safety. Employers must provide safe working environments in terms of safe work places and safe systems of work. This includes a requirement for a written policy, the identification of the personnel responsible for the organisation of health and safety, and arrangements for carrying out the policy. Schools should develop and apply their own policies for health and safety, based on the policy of their employer.

Health and safety is integral to good management. Head teachers have a responsibility for everything over which they have control. This includes all day-to-day health and safety issues, whether organised in curriculum time, out-of-hours sessions, at weekends or even during holidays. Where they do not have control, such as in aspects of capital finance, they are expected to take all reasonable measures to minimise problems. Subject leaders are responsible for health and safety issues within subject areas. Class teachers are expected to know and apply school policies, report shortcomings to senior management and take reasonable steps to control existing risks.

Employers cannot transfer responsibility for health and safety but may delegate, where appropriate, the necessary tasks in order to discharge the responsibility. It is at this level that teachers of physical education and school sport are involved in matters of health and safety – in carrying out risk assessments, interpreting the policy within physical education and school sport, informing others of the risks, and taking part in any appropriate professional development.

The health and safety of employees and non-employees, such as pupils and other visitors, must be safeguarded so far as is *reasonably practicable*. This means that the level of risk should be balanced against the cost of reducing that risk. Measures to reduce or eliminate risk must be taken unless the cost of doing so is obviously unreasonable compared to the level of risk involved. However, the balance must be firmly on the side of health and safety.

The issue of risk measured against cost was highlighted in a tribunal dismissal of an improvement order against Cardiff Ice Rink in 1997, in which protective netting was ordered at each end of the rink because spectators had been injured occasionally when the puck flew over the three-metre-high protective Perspex barrier. In dismissing the improvement order, the tribunal weighed the risk of injury against the possible loss of television revenue caused by the net impeding camera coverage; the subsequent loss of sponsorship if television coverage was lost; the supporters being against the proposal because it would impede viewing; there being no other practical alternative; the time and cost involved; and the offer for spectators to change seats if they so wished.

The statutory duties in health and safety are similar to those relating to negligence (responsibility, carelessness and foreseeability), with the essential difference that injury must be evident for liability in negligence, but exposure to the risk is sufficient for action under health and safety statute.

The Management of Health and Safety Regulations 1999 requires that risk assessments be carried out and recorded where there are more than five employees. This requirement may concern those involved in the teaching of physical education and school sport if they believe that the risk assessment record is binding, rather than it being simply a record of forethought and procedure pertaining at a particular time.

Risk assessments are nothing more than systematic general examinations of the people involved, environmental factors and workplace activities, which will enable those responsible to identify the risks posed by competence, working methods, processes, equipment and environmental influences. Having identified the hazards and determined the degree of risk, action may be required to reduce a high level of risk to a reasonable level.

3.5 OFFENCES AGAINST THE PERSON: VIOLENCE IN SPORT

Injuries occur in sport due to bad luck, careless acts or unacceptable violence on the pitch. Violence in sport may cause injury inflicted outside the laws and spirit of the game. The law establishes that committing assault, the real fear or actual infliction of force, is not allowed in sport other than in boxing, which has become an accepted exception. Dangerous play in sport represents unacceptable risk.

There is now case law evidence to suggest that this issue is not confined to adult participation. Thus, it is relevant to school staff, coaches and managers in school situations because they have what is known as a *secondary liability* for the actions and behaviour of the pupils on the pitch. This is because they were the last people to place the pupils in a competitive situation.

Criminal law requires evidence of the intention to commit the act, as well as evidence of the actual act that resulted in the injury being caused. Recklessness (ie harm not being directly intentional but knowing that the act may cause injury and continuing with it anyway) is interpreted as intent to cause injury. Many players have been fortunate to avoid criminal charges for wilfully causing injury to an opponent because it has been difficult to gather evidence of their intention to cause injury.

R v Moore 1898 (*14 TLR 229*) established that extreme violence resulting in death would automatically involve the police. Lesser outcomes of violent action in sporting events are rarely reported to the police. These outcomes are covered by the Offences Against the Person Act 1861 and include assault, actual bodily harm, malicious wounding, grievous bodily harm and manslaughter, each requiring proof of intent as well as proof of the actual act that caused harm. The escalating severity of the charge, from assault to manslaughter, is determined by the severity of the injury incurred. The Offences Against the Person Act 1861 involved the collation of a wide range of separate, existing statute dealing with violence. It is currently being reviewed with a view to creating statutes more relevant to modern society.

Significant similarities exist between criminal liability and the civil wrong of trespass, as both require evidence of intent, but the civil wrong is determined on a lower standard of proof and results in compensation to the claimant rather than a fine or custodial sentence.

3.5.1 Defences against criminal liability for violence in sport

The following guidelines can be of great value when refuting allegations of criminal liability for violence in sport.

3.5.1.1 Consent
Any requirement to prove intent, wilfulness or recklessness is complicated by the defence of consent to the likelihood of physical injury. Consent to battery is deemed to occur by the very act of participating in the game. However, it was shown in *R v Brown 1993* (*2 All ER 75*) that consent to the risk of injury is assumed only within the laws and spirit of the game. Criminal liability is necessary to provide some sanction when reckless violence is of such a degree that the referee's or sport governing body's ultimate sanction is inadequate for the severity of the crime.

3.5.1.2 Vicarious liability
Vicarious criminal responsibility is based upon the link between the offender and the teacher, coach or manager. Liability involves knowingly and deliberately encouraging or assisting someone else to commit an offence. If this is shown, prosecution may follow under the Accessories and Abettors Act 1861.

There are, as yet, no reported cases of criminal vicarious liability in physical education and school sport in the UK, but it could occur if a team manager has knowledge of a pupil's proven violent sporting offences, yet encourages the offender to participate. This may become evident if the manager continues to select the pupil with no effective requirement to desist from violent play.

Teachers or coaches who teach, encourage or accept over-aggressive play may be held liable if their players go beyond the rules and spirit of the game. This was outlined in *Nydegger v Don Boscoe Preparatory High School (Canada) 1985*. Secondary responsibility applies to teachers and coaches specifically in a school context, as they are the last adults to place the pupils in that situation. Any failure to exercise control over a team is the responsibility of the team manager; this is a responsibility the manager cannot afford to ignore, although, with no case precedent in the UK, the responsibility of team managers may require further clarification than commonly exists at the moment.

3.6 SAFEGUARDING CHILDREN IN PHYSICAL EDUCATION AND SCHOOL SPORT

Adults working with children are in positions of great moral and legal responsibility. Occasionally, this responsibility is undermined by the adult's actions. The most serious instance is when children are abused, particularly in a sexual way. Supervising pupils in physical education and school sport provides access to changing rooms, seeing children partially clothed, and creates the possibility of physical contact.

Systems and procedures exist in schools to provide effective protection for young people. National governing bodies of sport, Sport England and sports coach UK have produced helpful literature. Schools need to be aware of child protection requirements and have effective systems in place. Those with sole access to young people should be vetted by the Criminal Records Bureau before being allowed to work in such a position.

Legislation exists that seeks to prevent unsuitable adults working with children. The Protection of Children Act (POCA) 1999 and the Criminal Justices and Court Services Act 2000 are just two examples.

Where abuse has occurred, a wide range of specific statute may be brought into consideration. With the introduction of the Sexual Offences Act 2003, it is now an offence to groom young people for potential abuse (as in the manner described in Case 112, page 248).

Chapter 4
Good Practice Principles Identified from Case Law

The advice in Chapter 4 does not constitute a definitive list of good practice principles. For such advice, the reader is directed to *Safe Practice in Physical Education and School Sport* (baalpe, 2004)[1] . This chapter is simply a collation of the issues presented in the summarised cases in Chapter 5 and the information given here is listed under the appropriate headings of the model in Chapter 2 (Figure 2, page 16).

Readers are recommended to consider whether or not they apply these good practice principles to their own circumstances. The relevant case summaries in Chapter 5 (indicated at the end of each point) provide additional detail on the context from which each issue has been identified.

4.0 GOOD PRACTICE RELATING TO PEOPLE

4.0.1 Teachers, coaches and other responsible adults

4.0.1.1 Duty of care
School staff have a duty to take positive steps in order to protect pupils from physical harm. A judge, quoting the *Beaumont* and *van Oppen* cases (Case 67 and Case 93), said that 'school children, whatever their ages, are, in principle, within the protective pale of a teacher for whom an education authority is responsible' (Case 1). It should be noted that school staff responsible for pupils have a higher duty of care than parents responsible for family and friends (Case 2). Teachers, coaches and responsible adults should consider the following:

- Appropriate action must be taken when in possession of *guilty knowledge* (ie that which may cause harm to others) in order to reasonably prevent injury occurring. (Case 8)

- Curricular and voluntary sport must be properly authorised and organised by the school. (Case 13)

- Schools have a duty of care to ensure that competent adults teach, supervise and officiate sport activities, whether as part of curricular or out-of-schools-hours activity. (Case 13)

[1] British Association of Advisers and Lecturers in Physical Education (baalpe). (2004) *Safe Practice in Physical Education and School Sport.* Leeds: Coachwise Solutions. ISBN: 1 902523 68 7.

- School staff must educate pupils about the duty of care pupils owe their fellow players. (Case 22)

- The organisation and presentation of lessons should be based on *regular and approved practice* – that which has been used widely and over a sufficient period of time, and is therefore shown to be safe if organised properly. (Case 29 and Case 70)

- Regardless of the nature and level of the programme, school staff are expected to only allow activities that reasonably suit the level of ability of each individual involved. The courts generally recognise that no activity is inherently unsafe in itself. (Case 29 and Case 93).

- If play is within the laws of the game, players will not be held liable for injury to spectators. (Case 31)

- Children should be educated in their own safety and made aware of what they should consider when establishing safe working environments and implementing safe working practices. (Case 33)

- Pupils acting on behalf of their school, or representing their school for the school's benefit, may be deemed to be the responsibility of the school if behaving in a negligent manner, whether or not an employee (eg a teacher) is liable during the incident. (Case 34)

- All parties have a duty to inform others of possible dangers that may affect those involved and, where it is within their control, to make alternative arrangements in order to avoid the danger. (Case 41)

- Once school staff become aware of anything that threatens the safety of pupils in their care, action must be taken to remove or reduce the risk to an acceptable level. (Case 41)

- Anyone given a task must ensure that it is carried out or that failure to do so is reported. (Case 48)

- Staff should recognise that management involves monitoring and not simply delegation. (Case 48)

- A duty is owed to trespassers if a risk or danger is known or is reasonably foreseeable. (Case 62)

- Schools maintain the responsibility to ensure that pupils are not exposed to unacceptable levels of risk, whether or not school staff are directly responsible for leading the activity. (Case 74)

- Schools are required to provide proper supervision of potentially harmful situations and to take sensible precautions. (Case 82)

- As established in an early case (*Barfoot v East Sussex DC 1939* – see Case 3) it is incumbent upon school staff to highlight risks and warn against them. (Case 84)

- School staff are responsible for the acts of pupils participating in games, as the particular staff member responsible is the last adult to place the pupils in that situation. (Case 105)

4.0.1.2 Contract/insurance

The employer (LEA/governors/trustees) is responsible for what is authorised and the way in which it is carried out (Case 2). Tutors, coaches and responsible adults should consider the following:

- Due to the wide range of additional activities in which school staff often become involved, it is essential for members of staff to clarify whether they are working within the course of their employment, or participating in a private capacity in which they possibly have permission to use particular facilities. Such situations may include outdoor activities, trips or holiday sports coaching courses held on the school grounds. Working within one's course of employment involves:
  - the head teacher's knowledge and approval of the event and confirmation that the event is official
  - possible school governing body approval for the event, which is usually communicated through the head teacher. (Case 20)

- School staff involved in sports activities that are not directly associated with the school (eg regional sports associations, delivering national governing body awards or working with independent groups) must be covered by appropriate third-party liability insurance. According to the circumstances, they should check whether this is provided by:
  - the LEA/Governors as an employer
  - the national governing body of sport
  - independent arrangements. (Case 20)

4.0.1.3 Expertise

Expertise, based on qualifications and/or experience, is vital when teaching or coaching an activity. Possession of a national governing body award does not guarantee possession of the skills required for leadership, organisation, or the ability to analyse situations in relation to safety or knowledge of progression. These skills should be monitored (Case 6). Tutors, coaches and responsible adults should consider the following:

- The practice of older children gaining experience by working with younger pupils (as is common in *Junior Sports Leader* and other courses), while being laudable, needs careful and close supervision, and should be used as supplementary support with a group. (Case 9)

- Those assuming responsibility for the safe supervision of a child or a group should be given adequate training and be monitored regularly. (Case 9)

- School staff, coaches and volunteers involved in physical education must:
  - be fully taught or prepared
  - have a level of expertise in all the activities they are required to teach
  - provide necessary progressive practices
  - check that pupils understand and have a reasonable knowledge of the activity
  - avoid situations in which injury is foreseeable. (Case 16)

- School staff should keep abreast of current guidelines and follow these where mandatory, or take account of appropriate guidance when carrying out risk assessments. (Case 64)

- Volunteers and coaches working with groups should be experienced in the demands of the age group, activity and environment before assuming sole charge. (Case 71)

- Military qualifications are specific to the needs of the military and may not be appropriate in terms of understanding young peoples' development and capabilities. When pupils attend military-organised events, school staff continue to be responsible for them. Staff must be satisfied with the standards and attitudes of the instructional staff. This also applies to the use of commercial companies, such as ski schools. (Case 71)

- Those deemed to be *specialists* should have a greater insight into the implications of their actions. Thus, they will be judged at a higher level of responsibility. (Case 76)

- Teachers and coaches of specialist forms of gymnastics should be appropriately qualified or trained. (Case 87)

4.0.1.4 Participation
School staff, coaches and responsible adults should consider the following:

- Adults may take part in lesson activities in order to demonstrate and develop elements of play in games. They should not, however, assume a full part in any game due to the differences in strength, fitness, speed and experience. It is foreseeable that it could cause injury if, in the excitement of the game, an adult performs, for example, a dangerous, high tackle. This judgment has caused schools to carefully reflect on the wisdom of *staff versus pupils* matches in any activity. (Case 128)

- Adults should think carefully before demonstrating by using pupils in competition against themselves. (Case 16)

4.0.1.5 Officiating
Accidents in supervised play are much less frequent than in unsupervised play (Case 32). School staff, coaches and responsible adults should consider the following:

- Referees and umpires who spot something incorrect must instruct and correct (as well as referee) as they have both a duty of care and a duty of control. This means that referees in school rugby matches are expected to assume much more responsibility for the welfare of the players than referees in matches at senior level. This is due to the differences between teams in levels of skill, fitness and maturity. (Case 13)

- It is the responsibility of teachers or managers of school teams (who are probably not refereeing) to intervene and consult referees, or even abandon matches, if they believe that serious injury is foreseeable due to a lack of stringent officiating. (Case 13)

- Staff should ensure that pupils play within the rules and culture of the game. (Case 23 and Case 107)

- Staff should carefully organise and supervise games and lessons, and must be strict and vigilant when refereeing. (Case 23 and Case 93)

- At competitive events where spectators are present, staff should ensure that an adequate distance exists between the spectators and the field of play. This, however, may not be possible in typical school-level matches where spectators may stand on the touchline. (Case 31)

- Staff and officials should adequately ensure that no spectators encroach onto, or beyond, the touchline. Where allowed to encroach, any subsequent injury to spectators may cause the official to be held responsible. (Case 31)

- Team managers on the touchline should immediately substitute or remove from play anyone exhibiting violent conduct, either on or off the ball. (Case 106, Case 107, and Case 110)

- The infliction of injuries during play may be considered accidental, but injuries inflicted *off the ball* must be deemed deliberate and may be deemed criminal. (Case 110)

- Late tackles and acts of obstruction or violence away from the point of play must be dealt with severely. This may include sending the offender from the field of play, if the incident is deemed sufficiently violent to cause serious injury, or to have been performed with reckless intent. (Case 110)

4.0.2 Pupils and participants

4.0.2.1 Age
School staff, coaches and responsible adults should consider the following:

- Greater care is required in the supervision of younger children, as their awareness of the implications of their actions is limited. (Case 9)

- Minors cannot assume responsibility for the actions of very young children who may be placed in their care. This is an issue relating to the responsibilities that may, wrongly, be placed on young people with leadership experience. (Case 73)

- The judge's suggestion that a child aged between eight and nine years cannot be expected to be fully aware of the extent of their own abilities (Case 84) indicates an expectation for adults to:
  - use carefully staged progressive practices
  - be vigilant in observation
  - communicate clearly with pupils regarding what they may or may not do. (Case 84)

- If clear warnings are given to a class, the adult may be absolved from liability. However, this depends on the age of the class and whether or not the class is known to be well behaved. Where warnings are given, they should be specific to the dangers involved in the particular activity. (Case 84)

4.0.2.2 Ability

School staff, coaches and responsible adults should consider the following:

- Pupils should be fully appraised of the safety issues relating to activities in which they are involved. Furthermore, they should be involved in their own safety, at a level commensurate with their age, through a programme of safety education. (Case 21)

- Games have evolved over time in order to accommodate players of different sizes. (Case 82)

- In representative matches, players are expected to have been taught the appropriate techniques. They should also be confident in their application against opponents, regardless of size. (Case 82)

- In teaching situations, it may be prudent to match size, experience, strength, skill and confidence in contact or weight-bearing situations, or where an accelerating projectile is involved. (Case 82)

- Pupils should not be taken, or allowed, into situations that are clearly beyond their level of competence. (Case 102)

4.0.2.3 Special needs

Depending on the disabilities and activities involved, it may be necessary to allow more time for less able participants to complete particular tasks. This may have subsequent safety and management implications. (Case 21)

4.0.2.4 Behaviour

School staff, coaches and responsible adults should consider the following:

- It should be assumed that pupils behaving poorly or irresponsibly are likely to repeat such behaviour. Staff should state the required level of behaviour and keep such pupils under close supervision. (Case 4)

- A code of conduct should be established before going on trips, in order to forewarn pupils of the level of behaviour expected. (Case 4)

- Staff/managers must insist that pupils play within the rules and culture of the game. Reckless play may result in legal action, in which the adult may be implicated as the person responsible for the pupils' actions. (Case 22)

- A single, *spur-of-the-moment, off-the-ball* outburst cannot be predicted but, when it happens, it is foreseeable that it may occur again. School staff/coaches should consider action in order to prevent repetition of the behaviour. (Case 105)

- Prior knowledge of pupils' dispositions and behaviour is important. (Case 104)

- School staff should insist that players, staff and parents accept the referee's decision without challenge. (Case 106)

- Parents and other spectators verbally or physically abusing others should be asked to leave the premises. Incidents should also be reported to the head teacher. (Case 106)

- Team managers have legal responsibilities for the behaviour of pupils, regarding the repetition of reckless or intentional acts outside the rules and spirit of the game. (Case 107, Case 108 and Case 109)

4.1 GOOD PRACTICE RELATING TO CONTEXT

4.1.1 Facilities

4.1.1.1 General
School staff, coaches and responsible adults should consider the following:

- The provision of a facility, with or without a charge being made, entails the responsibility of ensuring that it is adequately maintained and supervised if others are to use it. (Case 48)

- If the environmental circumstances vary during a particular activity, constant review of the initial risk assessment is necessary to ensure that the facility remains safe to use. (Case 58)

4.1.1.2 Adventure activities
Off-site visits have a very important role to play in the overall education of young people (Case 94). School staff, coaches and responsible adults should consider the following:

- When using activity centres, staff should check whether they are licensed under the Adventure Activities (Safety of Young Persons) Act 1995 and comply with the regulations arising from the Act. (Case 102)

- If licensing is not a requirement, it should be ensured that tutors' qualifications and levels of experience are adequate, that equipment is appropriate, and that risk management procedures have been implemented in order to provide proper safety systems. (Case 102)

4.1.1.3 Athletics

School staff, coaches and responsible adults should consider the following:

- Sand in landing areas must be the correct type of sharp sand – not builders' sand. (Case 35)

- Landing areas must be dug – not simply raked – before use, whether for use in lessons or before competition. (Case 35)

- Raking during periods of use must be sufficiently adequate to maintain level, soft, impact-absorbing surfaces for landing. (Case 35)

- There may be times during use when raking becomes insufficient to maintain safe landing areas and digging is therefore required. (Case 35)

- Pupils should be taught to recognise when sand pits have become compacted by impact and should be encouraged to ask for this to be corrected before they jump. (Case 35)

- Participants taking part in events that are bounded by walls should be advised and taught not to run into barriers at speed. Instead, they should conclude the race earlier and take the speed out of the finish by, for example, touching a line on the floor. (Case 36)

- Risk assessments should even be carried out for *fun* events and the findings should be acted upon. (Case 36)

4.1.1.4 Playing fields

School staff, coaches and responsible adults should consider the following:

- It is important to allow sufficient space between activity areas and boundaries onto private land. (Case 39)

- Where persons or property are exposed to real risks of being struck by items of sports equipment (eg javelin, discus, football, cricket ball) the need to provide reasonable warning and/or protective fencing should be considered. (Case 39)

- Playing surfaces must be reasonably flat. Slight undulations are acceptable. (Case 40)

- Playing areas must be checked regularly for depressions, undulations and other faults. It must then be decided whether it is reasonable to play fast-moving games involving sudden changes of direction and, possibly, the need to keep a ball under control. (Case 40)

- Systems should be established to regularly check areas used for playing games in order to ensure reasonable levels of provision for pupils are being maintained. If the areas are prone to holes, stones, broken glass, animal excreta or other problems, alternative areas need to be used. (Case 44 and Case 54)

- When organising spectator events, current guidelines for specific sports (eg athletics) should be followed. Where guidelines are not provided, experience and common sense should be used to determine a safe distance between the court/pitch and the spectators, according to the demands of the game. (Case 47)

- Eight young people have been killed by unsafe or insecure goalposts in the last 10 years. (Case 53)

- Regular checks should be made to ensure the stability, condition and security of goalposts – especially portable ones – throughout the period during which the posts are left erected. (Case 53)

- Where potential vandalism may be an issue, checks on facilities such as goalposts should be more frequent and particularly thorough. (Case 53)

- The Department for Education and Skills (DfES) provides criteria for *run-off* areas on pitches for all sports. These need to be recognised and adhered to for both indoor and outdoor sports, in order to provide a nationally accepted safe area of play. Where such space is not available, risk assessments are needed to determine whether, and in what ways, the activities need to be adapted to maintain a safe environment. (Case 54)

- The placing of mobile goals and other equipment (eg for gymnastics) requires careful thought in order to provide safe working areas that allow for unanticipated movement. (Case 54)

- The provision of padded protection around goalposts and similar equipment during the playing of rugby is good practice. (Case 54)

4.1.1.5 Gymnasia, multi-use halls and sports halls

School staff, coaches and responsible adults should consider the following:

- Technical guidance is available on *run-off* area dimensions. Where space allows, this should be followed. (Case 37)

- Where space does not allow for a sufficient *run-off* area, pupils should be warned and the situation should be closely monitored. (Case 37)

- Crossing activity areas when games are in progress should be avoided, unless it is certain that the activity has ceased and it is safe for both the players and the person encroaching on the playing area. (Case 37)

- Participants and visitors should be involved in their own safety by developing an awareness of their surroundings. (Case 37)

- If space is particularly limited, or designs have inherent risks such as doors opening onto the work area, warning notices may be advisable. (Case 37)

- Wet floors present foreseeable risks of injury to participants and must be dealt with before play commences or continues. (Case 41)

- In older premises, glass should be checked to ensure it complies with current gymnasia standards. (Case 42)

- It is important to take account of identified significant risks in the facility by limiting the area of work or type of activity, or by implementing other appropriate action. (Case 42)

- It should be ensured that, to the best of the responsible adult's knowledge, the facility is suitable for the activity. The surface, projections and space should be checked. (Case 43)

- If a particular situation is judged to be unsafe, the activity, organisation, facility or conditions should be changed in order to make it reasonably safe. (Case 43)

- Realistic, periodic checks based on a local awareness of the facility are essential. They should be especially rigorous when the facility is used only occasionally or there is an opportunity for damage to occur. (Case 45)

4.1.1.6 Swimming pools

School staff, coaches and responsible adults should consider the following:

- Adequate verbal, written and/or visual warning of reasonably foreseeable hazards in the facility should be provided to visitors (including pupils). (Case 56)

- Arrangements should be made for the removal, disablement or *locking out of use* of equipment or facilities that could foreseeably cause serious injury if used at all or without adequate supervision. (Case 56)

- Pupils and other visitors should be taught to recognise and anticipate hazards and to take self-initiated appropriate action, especially in the context of poolside warnings and advisory notices. (Case 56)

- Pupils are either directed or invited to take part in activities and a general duty of care is owed to them. This requires that they be forewarned of potential hazards, such as the risks of diving from springboards into shallow water. (Case 57)

- Pupils' ability to differentiate between real and apparent depths of water should not be relied upon. (Case 57)

- Adequate notices about the water depth in pools should be clearly displayed. Adequate warning, visually and verbally, should also be provided. (Case 59)

- Pools in which the condition of the water prevents a clear view of the bottom of the pool should not be used. (Case 59)

- Adults must act on behalf of young people when considering allowing them access to open water or other facilities. (Case 63)

- There is no legal obligation for owners/occupiers to take extreme measures to prevent use, beyond those established by the owner/occupier. (Case 63)

4.1.2 Equipment

4.1.2.1 General

In *Webb v Rennie 1865*, Judge Cockburn said that 'to continue to use defective equipment is prime facie evidence of neglect' (Case 101). School staff, coaches and responsible adults should consider the following:

- LEAs provide equipment of reputable and modern design that satisfies European Standards, as will most other providers. If school staff are in doubt about safety, for example during an off-site visit abroad or to a playground where the equipment appears to be very old, a risk assessment of the equipment should be carried out. (Case 32)

- Very young children should be provided with the opportunities to use appropriate equipment. (Case 32)

- If equipment or facilities are deemed to hold significant risks when used without supervision, access or use should be prevented until, or unless, supervision can be arranged. (Case 50)

- Repair, and the subsequent adequacy of the equipment, should be confirmed by an appropriate adult before being brought back into use. (Case 50)

- Frequent checking and maintenance of equipment and facilities are essential. (Case 58)

- Faulty equipment should be removed from use immediately. Precautions should be taken to prevent further use until it is adequately repaired or replaced. (Case 58 and Case 67)

- *Regular and approved practice* (or design) should be implemented. Careful thought should be given before adapting or improvising equipment as this weakens one's position in the event of an injury and the case going to court. (Case 60)

- It is important that pupils are taught the correct methods of using equipment or facilities, through close monitoring to ensure that the correct mode of use is maintained. (Case 60)

- A visual check of equipment and facilities used is advisable, whether on the school site or at another location, to monitor any possible deterioration or defect before pupils begin work. (Case 60)

- The equipment provided in schools by an LEA is appropriate for the needs of that type of school. Staff need to facilitate progressive, guided experience of the full range of available equipment. (Case 65)

- Equipment should be made secure outside lessons. This is most effectively achieved by locking facilities, storerooms and changing rooms. (Case 69)

- The plant, systems of work and procedures for health on site must be safe for both visitors and those working there. This is the responsibility of those *controlling* non-domestic premises (ie governors, head teachers and school staff). (Case 69 and Case 101)

- Equipment, facilities and systems of work should be checked regularly. Defects should be reported and the appropriate action should be taken. (Case 101)

- Equipment, facilities or systems of work affected by an improvement notice must be replaced, repaired or adjusted to fully satisfy the order. They should not be used again until they have been approved. (Case 100)

- Essential safety equipment should be used and no *short cuts* should be taken for convenience. (Case 103)

4.1.2.2 Play

School staff, coaches and responsible adults should consider the following:

- Current standards of play equipment are extremely high. (Case 49)

- The unsupervised use of large-scale play equipment by very young children is far more likely to result in injury than when such children are supervised. (Case 50)

4.1.2.3 Games

Using benches turned on their sides as targets or goals is very common. Usually, they are pushed against the wall so that pupils are unable to get behind them. The distance between the bench and the wall is the distinguishing factor in Case 70. The pupil was able to get behind the bench and stumble over it. (Case 70)

4.1.2.4 Gymnastics

Regular maintenance checks on equipment are required under the Provision and Use of Work Equipment Regulations 1992. This has implications for the annual inspection of gymnastic equipment. Regulation 6(1) states, 'Every employer shall ensure that work equipment is maintained in an efficient state, in working order and in good repair' (Case 49). School staff, coaches and responsible adults should consider the following:

- Serious injury may occur when, in performing a high-momentum landing, a pupil lands on the edge of a thick weight-absorbent safety mattress. The greatest care should be taken to avoid this. (Case 66)

- Weight-absorbent safety mattress landing areas should be of a sufficient size in order to avoid the need for gymnasts to adjust their positions. (Case 66)

- As pupils are both young and diverse in their skills, it is likely that schools allowing gymnastic equipment to be readily available without supervision will be negligent, regardless of the cautionary or prohibitive notices that have been displayed, and the previous instructions that have been given. (Case 69)

- Systems should be implemented in order to ensure that children are unable to place themselves in *exceptional danger* through avoidable access to potentially hazardous situations. For example, these situations may be avoided by locking or disabling trampolines and trampettes to prevent unauthorised use. (Case 72)

- It should be carefully considered whether races over equipment are advisable at any time. (Case 74)

- Springboards are not usual pieces of equipment for primary school gymnastics lessons. Such rebound equipment, if used, should be carefully introduced and managed. (Case 84)

- Mats should be appropriate to the activity taking place. Deep, soft, weight-absorbent mattresses are necessary where unpredicted and poorly coordinated landings or falls may occur when the body is travelling at speed. Conversely, these would be inappropriate for landing from simple vaults. Here, one-inch-deep tumbling mats are more appropriate. (Case 87)

4.1.3 Personal clothing, jewellery and protection

4.1.3.1 General
It is essential that staff are familiar with national governing body or other professional advice, for example, *Safe Practice in Physical Education and School Sport* (baalpe, 2004)[1]. The relevant guidance should be followed (Case 97).

4.1.3.2 Clothing and footwear
School staff, coaches and responsible adults should consider the following:

- Footwear should be checked from time to time so that pupils become educated in the issue of foot and floor traction. (Case 43)

- Appropriate clothing and protection must be worn for adventure activities. (Case 55)

- As well as clothing and footwear, the absence of sharp objects such as buckles should be checked. Long hair should be tied back and other safety issues should be checked before anyone is allowed to participate. (Case 97)

- It should be insisted that all performers wear non-slip socks or trampoline slippers when using the trampoline. (Case 97)

4.1.3.3 Jewellery
The wearing of jewellery poses a foreseeable hazard to individuals or others around them in physical education and school sport. School staff have a responsibility in this area (Case 92). School staff, coaches and responsible adults should consider the following:

- In order to minimise the potential of jewellery to be a foreseeable hazard in physical activity, the following steps should be taken:
  - All jewellery should be removed.
  - If the jewellery cannot be removed, the situation should be made safe, for example, by adjusting the activity for the individual or group.

[1] British Association of Advisers and Lecturers in Physical Education (baalpe). (2004) *Safe Practice in Physical Education and School Sport*. Leeds: Coachwise Solutions. ISBN: I 902523 68 7.

- If the situation cannot be made safe, the individual should not participate.
- Body jewellery may be hidden. Pupils should be asked at the beginning of lessons if they are wearing body jewellery. If disclosed, the previous principles should be applied. If there are no admissions, the lesson may proceed as planned. If teachers become aware of any body jewellery being worn during the lesson, they should apply the above principles as soon as they become aware of the situation. (Case 92)

- Taping over studs is sometimes used as a strategy to make the situation safe. Such practice:
  - may not be effective if the individual's ear could potentially be struck forcibly by a ball or flailing arm
  - requires a clear decision to be made regarding who applies and removes the tape (ie the staff, pupil or other adult)
  - is subject to the fact that whoever applies the tape, the teacher, coach or other adult remains responsible for the effectiveness of the strategy. (Case 92)

- Any willingness on the part of parents to indemnify the school staff should be ignored. Indemnities have no legal status as pupils may bring retrospective action within three years of reaching adult age. (Case 91 and Case 92)

4.1.3.4 Personal protection
School staff, coaches and responsible adults should consider the following:

- The inclusion of a very good, fast bowler in a cricket team indicates the need to have appropriate personal protection to hand to use when necessary. If there is any doubt, cricket helmets should be worn. (Case 64)

- Mandatory requirements to wear mouthguards at junior international level to county level are set out by national governing bodies for sports such as rugby and lacrosse. Other national governing bodies advise such precautions. (Case 91)

- It is essential that parents are sent written information informing them that mouthguards are either mandatory or advisable for participation in games. Simply telling the pupils is clearly insufficient. (Case 91)

- Each school should have a written policy about the use of mouthguards and other personal protection and should ensure that it is applied consistently. (Case 91)

- In some schools, a mandatory requirement for mouthguards will have little affect on levels of pupil participation. However, in others it will decimate participation if the cost for individually fitted protection is too high for families to afford. Boil and bite mouthguards can cost as little as a few pence, may be *re-boiled and refitted* as the pupil grows, and certainly provide better protection than no mouthguard at all. Individually fitted mouthguards provide the best protection as they are thicker and spread the force of a blow more widely. However, these are much more expensive. (Case 91)

- Schools may establish mandatory or advisory policies on the wearing of mouthguards. In either instance, parents should be fully informed of the implications. It falls to the adult in charge of an activity to ensure that the situation remains safe for those taking part. Where mandatory, allowing pupils to participate without a mouthguard is in breach of the policy. Where advisory, it remains the responsibility of the adult in charge to ensure that the activity is safe and that the likelihood of injury is minimal for pupils without mouthguards. This may mean adjusting the activity to minimise such likelihood. The correct methods of teaching technical skills, and adequate supervision to avoid overly boisterous play, are also essential. (Case 91)

- Where parents provide such personal protection, schools need to ensure that changes to the curriculum at short notice do not place pupils at risk of injury because they have not brought the appropriate items of personal protection to school with them. (Case 91)

- Parental indemnification of the school for injuries sustained by children through not wearing mouthguards could be nullified if the children, on reaching adulthood (18 years of age), choose to initiate retrospective claims in their own right. (Case 91)

4.1.4 Procedures

4.1.4.1 Accident and emergency action

School staff, volunteers and coaches have a duty to take positive steps to protect pupils from physical harm (Case 1). They should consider the following:

- Schools need to have clear procedures for dealing with situations requiring first aid. These need to be understood and applied by the school staff. (Case 1)

- If a first aid situation appears to be escalating, an ambulance should be called as soon as possible. (Case 1)

- It should be ensured that clear post-accident procedures are followed. (Case 5)

- Contemporaneous notes on accident report forms are essential. In *Marshall v Bolton 1999* which concerns a road traffic accident, the judgment turned on the evidence of a witness who wrote a formal description just 10 minutes after the event. If a delay occurs, it is helpful to obtain a corroborative opinion or explanation from a reliable source. (Case 6 and Case 10)

- It is helpful to record all accidents and, when deemed good practice, to adjust organisation and management techniques. (Case 66)

- Accident report forms should be completed with clarity and detail. Diagrams and additional notes may prove to be advantageous and are considered good practice. (Case 68)

- In an emergency, the person in charge should balance the risks involved with the options that are available. (Case 76)

4.1.4.2 Dismissal

Parents should be informed of when and where groups will be received and dismissed, and where responsibility for the children is taken from, and handed back to, the parents. (Case 10)

4.1.4.3 Supervision
School staff, coaches and responsible adults should consider the following:

4.1.4.3.1 General
- Adequate supervision is necessary in order to monitor behaviour. (Case 27)
- Effective supervision is essential when pupils are involved in any activity that is deemed to be potentially hazardous. (Case 69)
- The law does not require pupils to be supervised every minute of the day but effective supervision is essential. (Case 89)
- Only in extreme circumstances should the responsible adult leave the class. No activity should be allowed while they are absent. (Case 89)
- School staff should make parents aware of when their children are the responsibility of the parents and when the staff assume responsibility for an organised event. (Case 95)
- Supervision that is adequate to the demands of the activity, and the age, ability and experience of those involved is essential. (Case 103)

4.1.4.3.2 Abuse
- It is important to recognise that physical, sexual and emotional abuse are closely related. (Case 112)
- All children have the right to protection from abuse. (Case 112)
- All suspicions of abuse should be taken seriously and responded to quickly and appropriately. (Case 112)
- Staff should learn to recognise the signs of abuse. (Case 112)
- Allegations of abuse are difficult to refute. Procedures should be established in order to avoid situations, whenever possible, in which a member of staff is alone with a pupil. (Case 112)
- Parents should be kept informed of supervisory arrangements. (Case 112)
- Procedures should be established regarding physical contact and support, which cannot be misconstrued. (Case 112)
- It should be ensured that the employer's requirements for disclosure certification are completed before anyone begins to work with pupils. (Case 112)
- It is important that staff liaise with the person in school who is responsible for child protection procedures. (Case 112)

4.1.4.3.3 Adventure activities

- It is vital to keep the issue of security on school journeys under constant review. (Case 52)

- Accommodation and security arrangements should be checked during pre-visits. (Case 52)

- It is advisable to have the whole pupil group in adjoining rooms, with staff quarters adjacent to these. (Case 52)

- Staff access to pupils' rooms must be available at all times. (Case 52)

- Staff should try to ensure that the accommodation area is for sole use by the group. (Case 52)

- Staff should establish whether 24-hour reception staff are available. (Case 52)

- In order to deter unauthorised visitors, the security arrangements should be checked and the school should be prepared to compensate the system by the use of school staff. (Case 52)

- It is useful to obtain a floor plan of the area designated to the group in advance. (Case 52)

- Staff members must acknowledge and understand the dangers, and accept the risk involved in adventure activities. They should not seek to off-load responsibility onto others. (Case 75)

- Members of staff who are responsible for young (and possibly inexperienced) pupils should check all equipment, facilities and conditions before and during the activities. (Case 75)

- Risk assessment and contingency planning are essential to the preparation of adventure activities. (Case 76)

- Risk assessments should be carried out for all adventure activities. Contingency planning for an alternative programme should also be prepared, in case the environmental conditions on the day require this. (Case 100)

- Appropriate safety equipment should be readily available during all adventure activities. (Case 100)

- Advice from experienced personnel should be considered seriously. (Case 100)

- The wisdom of including younger pupils in an activity that has been planned to be challenging for older pupils must be questioned. (Case 100)

- The inclusion of family members in a party should be questioned. It may deflect the adult member of staff from professional duties. (Case 100)

4.1.4.3.4 Games

- The issues of fair play and sportsmanship should be emphasised. (Case 108)

- The adult in charge should be pro-active when educating and enforcing the laws and spirit of the game. (Case 109)

4.1.4.3.5 Gymnastics and trampolining

- Close supervision is required of activities using rebound apparatus, such as trampolines or trampettes. (Case 89)

- Pupils in support/catching capacities should be taught effectively, monitored regularly and matched according to physique and strength. (Case 89)

- The competence of a performer in a specific task should determine whether the coach is situated on the trampoline itself, or standing alongside it. (Case 97)

- Up-to-date knowledge and practice in supporting is required. (Case 99)

4.1.4.3.6 Swimming

- Prior to a visit to a swimming pool, levels of pool-side supervision need to be determined through a risk assessment, according to the specific circumstances at the pool. (Case 17)

- Lifeguards should constantly scan all areas of the swimming pool in order to remain alert to what is happening. Distractions, such as watching particular groups for extended periods of time, should be avoided. (Case 17)

- Attracting a member of staff's attention to an incident in a school situation should be explicit and within the normal operating procedures. (Case 17)

- Locally defined *adult to pupil* ratios for swimming instruction should be noted and observed. (Case 18)

- Those responsible for pupils are expected to inform the pupils about their own safety, to draw attention to hazardous acts and to more securely supervise areas of greater hazard. (Case 19)

- The ages and levels of experience of the young people involved should influence the level of supervision. (Case 32)

- When using a public pool, the following guidelines should be adhered to:
  - Safety equipment and signs should be checked to ensure that they are present and prominent.
  - The pool's safety regulations should be checked and, if necessary, staff should impose more specific and stringent requirements on the school group.
  - The group should be regularly reminded of the safety requirements.
  - Diving should not be allowed if the freeboard is greater than the common 20–30 cm.
  - The national guidelines that were established in 1990, following Case 61, should be stringently followed. The current Amateur Swimming Association guidelines should be checked for the necessary depths of water that are required for racing, shallow and vertical dives. (Case 61)

- The importance of notices indicating that a facility is closed or entry is prohibited, and notices relating to the facility (eg depth, no diving) cannot be over-emphasised. Also, if relevant, notices indicating that a potential hazard exists (eg low water level) are vital. (Case 62)

- Facilities that are *out of use* need to be securely locked and/or access prevented in other ways as far as is reasonably possible. (Case 62)

- Ongoing risk assessments are necessary if the conditions of pool usage change in school pools, especially during the holidays when trespass may occur. (Case 62)

- The following guidelines are taken from the subsequent *Fatal Accident Enquiry 97:6 (95)*, which concerns a fatality in a swimming lesson:

    - Adequate levels of supervision are essential, taking into account prevailing circumstances and situations that may arise.
    - All staff need to be aware of the *silent drowning* phenomenon.
    - Head counts and scrutiny of the bottom of the pool should be regular.
    - If glare is affecting vision, those teaching should regularly move in order to be able to see all areas of the pool without glare. If this is not possible, they need to ask whether the class should be in the water.
    - The adult in charge should know the class and ensure effective communication with pupils who may have limited hearing, understanding or command of English.
    - There is a need for comprehensive, written, understood and applied operating procedures and emergency action plans.
    - The LEA/school policy and guidelines for safe practice should be followed.
    - Safe ratios, based on thorough risk assessments, should be determined. (Case 104)

4.1.5 Documentation

School staff, coaches and responsible adults should consider the following:

4.1.5.1 General
- Records form an important part of the defence against allegations of negligence or poor management. This is particularly important with regard to the inspection and maintenance of gymnastic equipment in halls and gymnasia. (Case 46)

- Routines and procedures need to be established and followed in order to identify potential hazards and take appropriate action within an acceptable time period. (Case 46)

- Systems and procedures, as per school documentation, should be followed. If a system, procedure or duty cannot be implemented, senior management should be informed immediately. Compensatory action can then be initiated. (Case 67)

- Notes from parents remain active until:
  - cancelled by a further and more recent note
  - directly instructed otherwise by the head teacher, who has been notified of the details. (Case 80)
- If a responsible adult is suspicious of the authenticity of a parental note, the request made in the note should be followed regardless. The issue of authenticity should then be investigated after the lesson. (Case 80)
- It is important to check pupil medical records to ensure that pupils' fitness is at an adequate level in order to enable them to participate in particular activities. (Case 80)

4.1.5.2 Risk assessment

- A risk assessment of the site should be arranged. This should enable the school to anticipate possible problems and organise the group and activity accordingly. (Case 4)
- School staff should consider, and share examples of, *near misses* within the school's mode of practice. This helps to highlight hazards that are in danger of becoming significant risks in terms of the frequency of the event occurring, even though, at the time of the event, no one was actually injured. In these circumstances, a review of risk is worthwhile. (Case 38)
- Risk assessments, and other records, such as those relating to maintenance or similar injuries, should be kept for a few years. (Case 46)
- Consideration should be given to risk assessments of what may occur in a situation of trespass, in order to ensure that reasonably foreseeable trespass could be prevented. (Case 62)
- Risk assessment is necessary in order to judge the levels of skill involved in relation to the quality of the facility available. (Case 64)
- Risk assessments need to be carried out and regularly reviewed in order to accommodate any aspects where risk is deemed to remain. (Case 67)
- Pupils should be warned of specific hazards. Such warnings should not be simply left at a general level. This requires risk assessments to be carried out and regularly reviewed. (Case 70)
- Risk assessments should be carried out at the planning stage and should be constantly reviewed during an activity. (Case 71)
- Duty of care is a process requiring ongoing assessments of risk according to the circumstances. Good planning will do much to discharge a reasonable duty of care. (Case 94)
- The level of risk varies according to the activity and the challenge involved. This determines the level of planning necessary. (Case 94)
- Schools can demonstrate that all the issues have been considered in a documented risk assessment. (Case 94)

- It is essential to have health and safety procedures in place and to ensure that they are adhered to at all times. (Case 103)

- Young people need to be involved in their own safety from the earliest ages so that they can recognise potentially hazardous situations and respond appropriately. (Case 103)

4.1.5.3 Informing parents

School staff, coaches and responsible adults should consider the following:

- It is prudent to educate parents about personal injury insurance. The school should inform parents about the programme in which the pupils will participate and whether or not the school has taken out pupil personal injury insurance. If the school has pupil personal injury insurance, parents should be aware of the levels of insurance. Parents may then choose whether to take further action. (Case 93)

- Forewarning children and parents of hazards on the school site is important. (Case 95)

4.2 GOOD PRACTICE RELATING TO ACTIVITY ORGANISATION

4.2.1 Preparation

School staff, coaches and responsible adults should consider the following:

- Pupils should be fully aware of what they need to do when participating in a demonstration or performing a skill. (Case 16)

- Staff should ensure that pupils are sufficiently prepared, physically and technically, for the demands of any task set. (Case 74)

- It is good practice to enquire after the fitness of the individuals in the group, before moving on to a demanding activity in order to forewarn them of the demands of the particular activity. (Case 77)

- The context of the warm-up should be related to the forthcoming activity. Bizarre and hazardous activities, where the benefit is not clearly apparent, may result in a successful claim for damages. (Case 77)

- Activities should be within the known capabilities and experience of the pupils involved. (Case 80 and Case 84)

- Long-term non-participants should be closely monitored when they initially rejoin lessons. (Case 80)

- Tasks may need to be adjusted for some pupils if their previous performance has been prejudiced by absence or injury. (Case 80)

- Adequate warm-up and cool-down activities are particularly vital in high-level gymnastics. While scientific research is divided on the benefits of warm-up/cool-down, the possible benefit of warm-up on performance has been accepted by the courts. (Case 87)

4.2.2 Class management

School staff, coaches and responsible adults should consider the following:

- Constant observation of pupils' positions and actions is essential. (Case 3)

- Officiating and teaching within a game situation is common. The roles need not be separated, provided that vigilance and feedback is sufficient to maintain adequate pupil safety. (Case 3)

- In striking games, close fielding must always be monitored and an appropriate judgement must be made by the responsible adult when this occurs. (Case 3)

- Knowledge of pupils taken off site for any activity is essential. The responsible adult should know the group as much as possible. (Case 4)

- The propensities of the group should be known. The group's interest in the activity, and the potential hazards that exist, should be taken into account by staff before carefully considering whether to allow sub-groups or individuals to operate beyond a position of close control (ie within sight and sound). (Case 4)

- Children's early, free movement on apparatus should be closely supervised in order to monitor confidence and competence in basic movement. (Case 5)

- Choosing an activity to end the lesson, which is based on the skills practised during the lesson, is more focused and predictable than *free activity*. (Case 18)

- Multi-activity arrangement in a single facility requires effective management with clear areas of work, run-off space and clear arrangements for action, should anyone need to move into another working area for any reason. (Case 21)

- Allocating and monitoring appropriate space according to the demands of the activity is essential. (Case 27)

- Good positioning to enable the responsible adult to view the whole class, observation and analysis of what is happening plus appropriate intervention, if deemed to be necessary, are crucial. (Case 65, Case 79 and Case 83)

- Schools need to regularly review their procedures. (Case 69)

- Regular and approved practice should be followed. (Case 76)

- The responsible adult should ensure that pupils:
  - do not run at speed in confined areas/bottlenecks
  - are under control when running so they are able to stop or change direction in order to avoid collisions, particularly before being placed in any competitive situation. (Case 78)

British Association of Advisers and Lecturers in Physical Education (baalpe). (2004) *Safe Practice in Physical Education and School Sport*. Leeds: Coachwise Solutions. ISBN: 1 902523 68 7.

- The purpose of the activity should be clear and any possibility of the activity causing injury anticipated. (Case 78)

- The responsible adult must feel confident that the group has the ability to stop on command. (Case 78)

- Clear organisation and control within contact activities is important, as is the need to group individuals according to size, strength, experience and confidence. (Case 79)

- The judgment in Case 81 indicates the need to teach pupils technique and to provide clear reasons why pupils have been taught to perform these techniques and skills in particular ways. There is also a need to explain the hazard in not doing an activity as taught. (Case 81)

- The responsible adult should be aware of class management issues when controlling prescribed gymnastic movements, as opposed to creative gymnastic movements. The whole issue of standing by and supporting becomes very important – details of this can be found in *Safe Practice in Physical Education and School Sport* (baalpe, 2004)[1]. (Case 84)

- When carrying out general open-ended tasks, school staff/coaches are advised to:
  - regularly scan the class as it works
  - judge whether individuals appear to be confident and competent in their movement
  - focus individual responses that are observed within the experience and confidence of specific pupils
  - forewarn pupils of any potentially hazardous use. (Case 85)

- Classes should be introduced to new items of equipment and instructed how they may be used within the context of the work currently being undertaken. (Case 85)

- Specific skills should be tailored to individuals' needs, experience and confidence. (Case 85)

- It is advisable to gather the class round to discuss the correct techniques and demonstrate the salient points in order to consolidate understanding of the requirements to ensure safe performance. (Case 85)

- Initial organisation to provide a safe working environment needs to be regularly monitored to ensure that it remains safe. (Case 96)

- Games areas should be organised to ensure that *run-off* areas and accelerating projectiles do not create a likelihood of injury for others working on, and focused on, other playing areas. (Case 96)

- The implications of using differentiated equipment should be considered within the overall organisation of a group, in order to ensure a safe working environment. (Case 96)

- Effective communication between adults and performers is very important in order to be absolutely clear about what performers are to do during high-risk activity performances. (Case 99)

- Decisions should be based on observation and judgements on performance, rather than the possible persuasive nature of a performer. (Case 99)

4.2.3 Progression

School staff, coaches and responsible adults should consider the following:

- Careful thought and progressive build-up should be given when deciding whether a pupil's age, experience, and the fact that they have been warned of the risk involved, is appropriate to the degree of supervision provided by the adult responsible. Independence comes through experience and progress. (Case 2)

- Regular and approved practice should be followed, especially for situations involving progression and development. (Case 5)

- It is becoming increasingly common to establish systems of *opting out* of support rather than *opting in* to it, in order to ensure no misunderstandings and that pupils have the confidence to perform the task. (Case 7, Case 86 and Case 88)

- It is essential to check that procedures are followed and essential equipment is used. Even when groups are beginning to work independently, such requirements should be monitored and action taken if it is noticed that individuals make omissions. (Case 15)

- Following a gap between practice or lengthy absence from activity, the responsible adult should remind pupils to take things easy and revise the essential points before putting them into practice. (Case 15)

- It is important to provide appropriate progressive activities, cater for the individual's ability or needs, and be in a position of close supervision when a task new to a pupil is first attempted. (Case 20)

- Sufficient space, time and forewarning should be allowed according to the abilities of the pupils involved in an activity. Proficiency and consistency allows for less space than where a player's performance is not usually predictable. (Case 28)

- Chasing games, obstacle races and other competitive activities over gymnastic apparatus are not using the equipment for the purpose it was designed. (Case 68)

- It is foreseeable that competitive races or chasing games over apparatus, such as Pirates, place pressure on the pupils who, in haste, may fall from the apparatus. (Case 68)

- When mats are used to provide cushioned landing areas, stringent observation and action by staff and pupils who have been taught to handle such situations, are necessary to ensure that the mats are immediately repositioned should they move. This may require a temporary halt to the activity. (Case 68)

- Imposing forfeits for the last individual or group to finish a task (eg press-ups) has no educational value and creates an inappropriate, pressurised situation. (Case 68)

- A preview by pupils before any section of a particular challenge in an outdoor, adventurous activity is important so that they do not participate *blindly*. (Case 71)

- Activities should be carefully matched to levels of experience. (Case 71)

- Staff should not be afraid to say 'stop'. (Case 71)

- It is important to consider whether the placement of support will help or adversely affect the safety of the task. (Case 74)

- Pupils need to be psychologically prepared and confident of success when performing tasks. (Case 85)

- It should be considered whether it is wise for pupils receiving support on one task to progress to another related task without support. (Case 86)

- Responsible adults should think very carefully about whether supports or *stand-ins* are necessary. This tends to occur when movements are set and thus predictable, as in formal gymnastic skills rather than *free movement* planned by the performer. When a support or *stand-in* is available, very clear communication is necessary between the adult and the performer in order to ensure that no misunderstandings arise. The *stand-in* should be fully trained in the correct supporting techniques and should display a responsible attitude to the job. (Case 87)

- Even today, the principle applies to:
    - supporting pupils who are not very proficient
    - standing by when proficiency develops in case the pupil stumbles on landing
    - there being no need to stand by when the pupil has become proficient. (Case 88)

- It is advisable to establish a system where approved pupils may choose to work without support. (Case 90)

4.2.4 Technique

4.2.4.1 Adventure activities
School staff, coaches and responsible adults should consider the following:

- Skiers should be taught how to fall in order to minimise the likelihood of injury. (Case 55)

- Pupils should be taught techniques in order to minimise the likelihood of falling when skiing. (Case 55)

- School staff and coaches should be well experienced and, where possible, well qualified in activities which may be potentially hazardous to young people. (Case 75)

- Pupils need to progress through rigorous training and assessment processes before enjoying any degree of independence or responsibility, such as in leading a climb. (Case 75)

- The practice of short cuts should be avoided. (Case 76)

4.2.4.2 Games

School staff, coaches and responsible adults should consider the following:

- Good techniques should be reinforced with pupils. (Case 24)

- Pupils should be reminded that, in football, staying on one's feet rather than sliding into a tackle, is more likely to lead to keeping control of the ball after the tackle is completed. (Case 24)

- When working in a confined space, pupils should be taught to check the area into which they are about to propel any ball or other item before doing so. (Case 83)

- Pupils should have reasonable expectations of striking the ball accurately. (Case 83)

- The use of warning notices in confined spaces can be reasonably expected. (Case 83)

- More recent case law indicates that judgments have gone against the person striking the ball without a reasonable level of control. (Case 83)

- Pupils should be taught the necessary techniques, skills and rules to play games with reasonable safety, through experiencing appropriate, progressive practices. (Case 93)

4.2.4.3 Gymnastics

Tutors, coaches and responsible adults should consider the following:

- While there is no required technique for supporting gymnastic vaults, it is important to ensure that variations from what is commonly used are safe and effective. (Case 6)

- The pupils' ages, previous experience and training, behaviour and responsible attitudes should be considered before they are given the responsibility of supporting each other. (Case 29)

- School staff and coaches should read and follow the advice in *Safe Practice in Physical Education and School Sport* (baalpe, 2004)[1] on supporting and standing by. (Case 93)

- Great care should be taken when teaching technical skills. (Case 98)

- Progressive steps should be practised with reference to earlier learned practices where necessary. (Case 98)

- Checking pupil understanding at each stage of the correct and safe mechanics of any skill or part-skill is important. (Case 98)

4.2.4.4 Swimming

Tutors, coaches and responsible adults should consider the following:

- Underwater swimming/diving in shallow water should be properly taught. Pupils should be instructed to lead with their hands as they approach the bottom of the pool. (Case 18)

- Risk management should be undertaken with the pupils, so that they are aware of any hazards and how these may be properly avoided. Risks include striking the bottom of

[1] British Association of Advisers and Lecturers in Physical Education (baalpe). (2004) *Safe Practice in Physical Education and School Sport*. Leeds: Coachwise Solutions. ISBN: 1 902523 68 7.

the pool, striking a side wall of the pool and closing their eyes underwater. (Case 18)

- Young people should be taught to assess the circumstances of their environment and activity before committing themselves to an action. They need to be attentive to the task in hand. (Case 59)

- Running dives should not be allowed in class situations and should be strongly discouraged in leisure situations. Running dives do not allow adequate time for performers to assess the situation and amend their intended action before being committed to it. (Case 59)

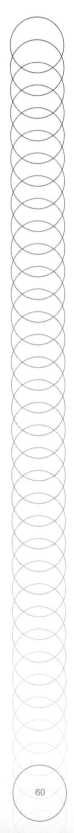

Case Law in Physical Education and School Sport:
A Guide to Good Practice

Chapter 5
Analysis of Case Law to Identify Issues for School Staff, Coaches and Volunteers

5.0 INTRODUCTION

The cases outlined in this chapter are organised into the following sections:

5.1   Cases of Negligence Relating to People: School Staff, Coaches and Volunteers

5.2   Cases of Negligence Relating to People: Pupils and Participants

5.3   Cases of Negligence Relating to Context: Facilities

5.4   Cases of Negligence Relating to Context: Equipment

5.5   Cases of Negligence Relating to Activity Organisation: Preparation

5.6   Cases of Negligence Relating to Activity Organisation: Teaching and Organisation

5.7   Cases Relating to Health and Safety

5.8   Cases Relating to the Offences Against the Person Act 1861: Violence in Sport

5.9   Cases Relating to Child Abuse in Sport

In each section, cases are arranged according to:

- activities
- ages or phases
- alphabetical order of the claimants' names
- the year in which the cases were heard in court.

Overleaf is an example of the layout of each case in Chapter 5.

Case Law in Physical Education and School Sport:
A Guide to Good Practice

Case

Activity:
Age:
Principle:

> **NAME OF CLAIMANT _v_ NAME OF DEFENDANT**
> **Court and year in which case was heard**
> **Law report abbreviation (where readily available)**
> **Source of transcript or summary**

Summary:

An outline of the facts of the case.

Judgment:

The judge's reasoning and decision.

Issues to consider:

Relevant principles that should be considered in planning and practice.

NB Unreported cases do not have a source of transcript or summary.

Case Law in Physical Education and School Sport:
A Guide to Good Practice

5.1 CASES OF NEGLIGENCE RELATING TO PEOPLE: SCHOOL STAFF, COACHES AND VOLUNTEERS

Case 1

Activity: Asthma attack
Age: Secondary
Principle: Positive action to protect from harm

HIPPOLYTE v BEXLEY LONDON BOROUGH
Court of Appeal (Civil Division), 1994
Transcript: John Larking
Lexis

Summary:

- A 16-year-old asthmatic suffered brain damage following a severe attack while at school. She had already been hospitalised on three occasions in seven months as a result of asthma attacks.

- The claimant's mother alleged that due care would have avoided brain damage.

- The claimant used her inhaler during the lesson but her condition did not improve. The teacher suggested that the claimant went home three times during the lesson but she refused. The claimant also resisted pressure to go to the secretary's office.

- The teacher then left the lesson to inform the secretary. On the way, she met a member of senior management, who said that the claimant was to go to the secretary immediately with a note from the teacher. Two pupils were elected to accompany the claimant. She collapsed twice on the short journey and her condition worsened despite using her inhaler.

- The claimant was eventually carried to the office by a teacher and an ambulance was called. The ambulance crew administered oxygen approximately 40 minutes after the teacher first told the claimant to report to the secretary's office.

- The teacher admitted, soon after the attack began, that an ambulance would be needed, but it was not called for a further 30 minutes. This is an issue of foreseeability. The teacher also said she did not know that a victim of an asthma attack could suffer injury.

- The LEA argued that there was no duty of care owed to someone over the age of 16 to take positive steps to get medical help, if the pupil developed health problems on school premises.

Judgment:

- The claim was dismissed in the first instance. This judgment was reinforced at appeal.

- It was specifically found that the oxygen was administered approximately five minutes too late. If the ambulance had arrived earlier, and had the expert first aid attention been available immediately, brain damage would not have occurred.

- The situation escalated from concern to anxiety and, eventually, to serious alarm. At this point, the action taken was appropriate and an ambulance was called.

- It was found that the claimant resisted efforts to persuade her to go home.

- No suggestion of deliberate delay or indifference was found.

- The Court of Appeal found that the school's action as the situation escalated was as much as could be reasonably expected.

- The argument that an LEA owes no duty by law to take positive steps to get medical help for a pupil over the age of 16 was severely criticised. It was confirmed that a teacher has a special relationship with a pupil.

Issues to consider:

- School staff, volunteers and coaches have a duty to take positive steps in order to protect pupils from physical harm. The judge, quoting the *Beaumont* (Case 67, page 204) and *van Oppen* (Case 13, page 90) cases, said that 'school children, whatever their ages, are, in principle, within the protective pale of a teacher for whom an education authority is responsible'.

- If a first-aid situation appears to be escalating, an ambulance should be called as soon as possible.

- Schools should have clear procedures for dealing with situations requiring first aid. These procedures need to be understood and applied by school staff.

- School staff, lecturers and recreation assistants need to know the full issues of duty of care for students over the age of 18 and in the care of schools, colleges or sports centres. A responsibility for people over the age of consent still exists.

Case 2

Activity: Athletics
Age: Secondary
Principle: Inadequate supervision

> **PORTER _v_ LONDON BOROUGH OF BARKING and DAGENHAM**
> **Queen's Bench Division, 1990**
> _The Times_, **9 April 1990**
> **Lexis**

Summary:

- Two 14-year-old boys (one of whom was the school caretaker's son) were allowed by the caretaker to take a shot onto the field after the school had closed for the day. They wanted to practise shot putting for the school sports day.

- The boys were joined by a 20-year-old and a child aged three. The 20-year-old joined in and, as he putt the shot, the three-year-old ran onto the field. To protect the infant, the 14-year-old visitor ran after him. The 14-year-old was subsequently hit on the head by the shot and suffered a seriously fractured skull.

- The injured boy claimed negligence on the part of the caretaker for allowing access to the shot. He also claimed vicarious liability on the part of the LEA, suggesting that the caretaker's actions were within the course of his employment.

Judgment:

- Both claims were dismissed.

- The court held that the caretaker had effectively provided the shot for the two boys and had expressly permitted them to use it. However, the opinion of the school's head of department that 'in no circumstances whatever should two 14-year-olds be allowed to use a shot to practise together...unsupervised' was rejected. It was held to insufficiently indicate the standard of care required of parents in charge of children under the circumstances and was described by Justice Simon Brown as 'perfectionist, unattainable and not sensibly to be imposed in day-to-day domestic life'.

- Furthermore, it was held that it is important not to stifle a measure of initiative and independence on the part of the growing boys. The judgment was given that the common organisation for a class (with half throwing simultaneously on command and the other half stationed safely behind) may need a 'degree of regimentation in school life, with a variety of children, some more responsible than others, and with the teaching staff understandably putting the very highest premium on safety'. However, it was also recognised that 'those standards...are certainly not to be expected by parents'.

- The LEA was not held vicariously liable because the event took place outside the caretaker's employment. It was deemed to be 'purely a family occasion' because it occurred well after the school had been locked up and in the caretaker's free time 'for his own private, domestic purposes – to perpetrate a flagrantly unauthorised act'.

Issues to consider:

- This judgment set out a higher duty of care for school staff with pupils than for parents responsible for family and friends. If the lack of supervision had occurred during a taught lesson, the inference is that the judgment would have been different.

- The need to clarify what occurs within and outside the adult's sphere of employment is reinforced in this case. An act in the course of employment is deemed wrongful if it is:
  - an authorised wrongful act
  - a wrongful and unauthorised mode of carrying out an unauthorised act.

- The LEA/governors are responsible for what is authorised and the way in which it is carried out. What needs to be established is whether the event is deemed to be an independent act because it is beyond being a mode of doing an unauthorised act.

- Careful thought should be given and progressive build-up provided when deciding whether a pupil's age, experience, and the fact that they have been warned of the risk involved, is appropriate to the degree of supervision provided by the adult responsible. Independence comes with experience and progress.

Case 3

Activity: Cricket
Age: Secondary
Principle: Teachers fulfilling dual roles

BARFOOT v EAST SUSSEX COUNTY COUNCIL
1939
The Head's Legal Guide, **Croner, pp 3–4**

Summary:

- During a cricket lesson, a pupil was injured while fielding close to the wicket. The injured pupil was said to be less than 9 m away from the bat.

- The teacher was reported to be acting in a dual role, as both teacher and umpire.

- The pupil claimed to have been placed at *silly mid on* (close to and facing the batsman) while the teacher claimed that the pupil was at square leg (at right angles to the wicket) and had moved close to the batsman of his own accord.

Judgment:

- The judge chose to ignore expert evidence supporting the teacher and awarded damages to the pupil.

- It was held that officiating prevented sufficient supervisory care being applied by the teacher.

- The situation was deemed to be dangerous, with a failure 'to exercise the care which the law required, from a master in charge of pupils in these circumstances'.

Issues to consider:

- Constant reinforcement of safety issues, as prescribed by the relevant national governing body, is necessary to ensure that pupils understand the issues.

- Constant observation of pupils' positions and actions in play and practice is essential.

- Officiating and teaching within a game situation is common. These roles need not be separated, providing that vigilance and feedback is sufficient to maintain adequate pupil safety.

- Close fielding must always be monitored and an appropriate judgement must be made by the responsible adult when this occurs.

- Pupils should be involved in developing a sense of risk. They should be made aware of the implications of their actions, commensurate with their age and ability.

Case 4

Activity: Field studies
Age: Secondary
Principle: Duty of care – inadequate supervision, control and organisation

PORTER v CITY OF BRADFORD MBC
Court of Appeal, 1985
Transcript: Association
Lexis

Summary:

- An appeal by the LEA against a decision at Crown Court in 1983 (at which the LEA was found to be negligent) was denied. The original Crown Court decision was upheld.

- A Year 11 pupil on a field studies visit to a local rocky area was injured.

- The accompanying teacher had not previously taught the group and did not know any of the pupils.

- Two pupils detached themselves from the group and began rolling boulders (large rocks) down a hill towards where the rest of the group was working.

- It was alleged that the teacher saw one of the pupils doing this and told him to stop, before moving approximately 50 m across the valley to a second group of pupils. This was out of sight and sound of the first group.

- The pupil who had been rolling rocks then began to throw rocks from a bridge onto a dry stream bed where the first group was working. He continued to do this for approximately 15 minutes.

- One of the rocks hit the claimant, fracturing her skull.

- The teacher did not give evidence, so the judge was unable to form an opinion of the teacher's attitude towards controlling and organising the group. The facts of the case were not disputed.

Judgment:

- There was no suggestion of contributory negligence by the claimant.

- The teacher was held to be clearly responsible for the safety of the group and, in the light of his being aware of the pupil's misbehaviour, negligent.

- The judge referred to the issue of duty of care and quoted *Williams v Eady 1893* regarding the careful parent test.

- The judge accepted that the teacher did not know the group as individuals. However, the judge also held that the teacher was aware of the pupil's 'propensity to do acts which might endanger fellow pupils by rolling these boulders down the slope in the sight of the teacher'.

The judge also said:

There were circumstances in which there was a foreseeable danger and that danger was obviously recognised by the teacher as he told the pupil to stop. Having had what I regard as a warning about the pupil's propensities, the teacher failed to exercise proper supervision over his party. He should have attempted to keep the group together, within, at any rate, sight and sound of him. The pupil's misbehaviour in a potentially dangerous way...should have been sufficient warning that the pupil was capable of dangerous and irresponsible actions and needed supervision. If the pupil had been kept in sight, the teacher would have known what the pupil had got up to again and would have taken steps to prevent it. The teacher failed in his duty to supervise this particular set of pupils.

Issues to consider:

- Knowledge of pupils taken off site for any activity is essential. The responsible adult should know the group as much as possible.

- It should be assumed that pupils behaving poorly or irresponsibly are likely to repeat such behaviour. Staff should state the required level of behaviour and keep such pupils under close supervision.

- A risk assessment of the site should be arranged. This should enable the school to anticipate possible problems and organise the group and activity accordingly.

- A code of conduct should be established before going on trips, in order to forewarn pupils of the level of behaviour expected.

- Teachers should know the propensities of the group, their interest in the activity and any potential hazards that exist before carefully considering whether to allow sub-groups or individuals to operate beyond a position of close control (ie within sight and sound).

- School staff should be prepared to question arrangements that are completely unable to meet acceptable levels of safe management. Health and safety law puts responsibility on employers (and thus head teachers and governors) for any deployment of adults into a situation for which they clearly lack the expertise and ability to provide a safe working environment.

Case 5

Activity: Gymnastics
Age: Primary
Principle: Adequate supervision

FELGATE v MIDDLESEX COUNTY COUNCIL
1954
The Head's Legal Guide, **Croner, pp 3–489**

Summary:

- A six-year-old girl was participating in a lesson on an apparatus arrangement that included two horizontal bars suspended approximately 1 m and 1.75 m above the ground. Mats were located beneath both bars.

- While sitting on the lower bar, the girl lost her balance, fell off and broke her arm.

- The parent alleged inadequate supervision by the teacher, who was close by attending to a boy who had climbed up a ladder on the same apparatus arrangement.

- The parent also criticised the post-accident procedures at the school. The child had been sent to hospital before her parents were informed.

Judgment:

- The claim was dismissed. It was held that neither the teacher nor the method of supervision was negligent.

- General supervision was adequate and the judge approved of young pupils being allowed to undertake free activities which encouraged independence.

- The teacher was deemed to have adopted a 'well-recognised practice'.

- The judge stressed the importance of calling immediately for an ambulance if skilled treatment is deemed necessary. The judge said, 'Children are happier if they have their mothers with them, but I think the presence of the mother before the ambulance is summoned is not nearly so important as the summoning of an ambulance'.

- This reflects the support for teachers taking emergency action as expressed in the Children Act 1989.

Issues to consider:

- Children's early, free movement on apparatus should be closely supervised in order to monitor confidence and competence in basic movement.

- Regular and approved practice should be followed, especially when dealing with progression and development.

- Clear, post-accident procedures should be followed.

Case 6

Activity: Gymnastics
Age: Primary
Principle: Teacher expertise

MILLS v STAFFORDSHIRE COUNTY COUNCIL
Stourbridge County Court, 2002

Summary:

- The claimant attended a gym club that was a satellite for a schools' centre of excellence.

- The claimant was practising headsprings, with support, from a static squat position on a box top placed lengthways. She alleged that she fell backwards and struck her head on the end of the box, damaging the upper spine.

- Two highly experienced subject leaders ran the gym club. The teacher in charge had up-to-date British Gymnastics (BG) qualifications, which enabled her to be in charge of such a club. She also tutored LEA in-service courses.

- The second teacher did not have BG qualifications but had in-depth experience from an initial teacher training course and subsequent in-service courses. She worked under the direction of the teacher in charge.

- The floor of the hall was completely covered with 25 mm matting. All five sections of the vaulting box were used with a weight-absorbent mattress beyond to cushion landings.

- The teacher asserted that the claimant had practised headsprings for approximately three weeks before the alleged incident, performing at least a dozen attempts successfully.

- The claimant alleged that, on her second or third attempt, she lost her balance when landing due to the second teacher's failure to provide the necessary support, thus hitting her head on the box.

- The other gymnasts did not recall seeing the claimant fall backwards.

- The teacher claimed that the gymnast had not fallen backwards and had not hurt herself, stipulating that a complaint had not been made until the following week. They had then completed an accident form retrospectively.

- The claimant alleged that:
  - the second teacher was not properly qualified to support the vault
  - the teacher's supporting technique was completely incorrect
  - the teacher did not move along the mat with her to ensure she received support during the vault
  - she was not ready to attempt the vault
  - the necessary progressive practices had not been covered.

Judgment:

- The claim was upheld on the basis that:
  - the teachers were guilty of a conspiracy, which included filling out a retrospective accident report
  - the teacher in charge should have monitored the second teacher's technique to ensure it was acceptable and consistent with that advised by BG.

Issues to consider:

- While there is no required technique for supporting gymnastic vaults, it is important to ensure that variations from what is commonly used are safe and effective.
- *Style* in the witness box is important. It was reported that the teachers were reticent and hesitant when giving evidence.
- Contemporaneous notes on accident report forms are essential. In *Marshall v Bolton 1999*, which concerns a road traffic accident, the judgment turned on the evidence of a witness who wrote a formal description just 10 minutes after the event. If a delay occurs, it is helpful to obtain a corroborative opinion or explanation from a reliable source.
- Expertise, based on qualifications and/or experience, is vital when teaching or coaching an activity. Possession of a national governing body award does not guarantee possession of the skills required for leadership, organisation, or the ability to analyse situations in relation to safety or knowledge of progression.

Case 7

Activity: Gymnastics
Age: Secondary
Principle: Inadequate supervision

GIBBS v BARKING CORPORATION
Court of Appeal, 1936
1 All ER 115
Lexis

Summary:

- The claimant stumbled while vaulting over a horse in a gymnastics lesson.

- The teacher was not in a position to support the claimant. It was held that 'the master did nothing to assist the boy in landing'. This fact was not disputed.

Judgment:

- The teacher was deemed not to have provided the level of care necessary. This was upheld at appeal.

- In this instance, it was held that 'it was the duty of the games' instructor to see that each boy, as he jumps over the horse and comes to the other side, does not fall...the games master does not seem to have acted with that promptitude which the law requires'. The terminology of the day should be noted.

Issues to consider:

- It is important to recognise that this took place in 1936, when formal gymnastics with regular teacher support was common. The judge's comments imply an expectation for all vaults to be supported.

- Today, teaching progressive practices and providing support where necessary is more common, with support being reduced and ultimately removed as confidence and expertise increases.

- It is becoming increasingly common today to establish systems of *opting out* of support rather than *opting in*, to ensure there are no misunderstandings and that pupils have the confidence to perform the task.

Case 8

Activity: Horse riding
Age: Adult
Principle: Failure to respond to *guilty knowledge*

> **STARLING v HOOGEMAN**
> **Queen's Bench Division, 1983**
> **134 NLJ 283**
> **Transcript: W.H. Clark**
> **Lexis**

Summary:

- An area of marshland near the Medway towns was let for the grazing of approximately 25 horses.

- The owners visited the horses to care for and ride them.

- When the claimant visited her horse, an unbroken horse blocked her access to the field through a gate. Therefore, the claimant entered the field over the fence some distance from the gate.

- As she walked through the field she heard a horse charging up behind her. It was the horse that had blocked her entry via the gate.

- The horse reared, smashing the inside of the girl's knee. It then stood over her and proceeded to kick her. Nothing had happened to provoke the attack.

- Another person in the field rescued the girl and she was taken to hospital.

- By law, the keeper of an animal not considered to be a dangerous species is liable for any damage caused by the animal.

Judgment:

- Attacks by horses are unusual.

- The owner was aware of the horse's aggression and underestimated the risk of someone getting hurt. This was deemed to be a misjudgement.

- The owner was found to be negligent. Even though the owner was aware of the horse's aggressive behaviour towards others, appropriate action was not taken to prevent an attack.

Issue to consider:

- Appropriate action must be taken when in possession of *guilty knowledge* (ie that which may cause harm to others) in order to reasonably prevent injury occurring.

Case 9

Activity: Play
Age: Pre-school
Principle: Inadequate supervision

> **BURTON v CANTO PLAY GROUP**
> **Queen's Bench Division, 1989**
> **Transcript: Laidler Haswell**
> **Lexis**

Summary:

- A timid girl aged three fell approximately 1 m onto grass when attempting to swing inside a geodesic dome climbing frame. She broke her arm and suffered some permanent loss of flexion.

- The adult staffing level at the playgroup was well within accepted ratios.

- A 14-year-old student on community service from a local secondary school was delegated to supervise the activity. The qualified staff did not offer training or specific instructions.

- The supervising student stepped back from the child, assuming that she was about to swing from the frame. However, the student failed to anticipate the outcome and the child slipped and fell. It was the child's first time on the climbing frame.

- A claim for negligence was made against the qualified staff for inadequate supervision.

Judgment:

- The climbing frame was deemed to be suitable for the age of the child.

- Adequate supervision was judged to be required due to the age of the child.

- It was recognised that there was the potential to cause substantial injury.

- It was held that possible injury was foreseeable and that safeguards were necessary to avoid such an occurrence, including relevant instruction to the supervising student.

Issues to consider:

- Greater care is required when supervising young children. Their awareness of the implications of their actions is limited.

- The practice of older children gaining experience by working with younger pupils (as is common in *Junior Sports Leader* and other courses), while being laudable, requires careful and close supervision.

- Pupils and students should not operate independently of qualified staff. Instead, they should be used as supplementary support with a group.

- Those assuming responsibility for the safe supervision of a child or a group should be given adequate training and should be regularly monitored.

Case 10

Activity: Play
Age: Primary
Principle: Responsibility for supervision

DEAN *v* MUNICIPAL MUTUAL ASSURANCE LTD
Court of Appeal, 1981
Transcript: Association
Lexis

Summary:

- An adventure playground consisted of swings, a slide and a seesaw.

- Two children, aged eight and 11, went to play on the apparatus while waiting for their father to collect them from another activity at a local centre.

- A member of staff, who had been involved in the earlier activity, offered to give the younger boy some *bumps* on the seesaw. During this, another boy jumped onto the adult's end of the seesaw, throwing the claimant into the air, thus breaking his front teeth on the end of the seesaw as he fell.

- The accident was logged in the centre's accident book but a detailed written report was not made.

- The claimant's father alleged that the seesaw was in an unsuitable position in the playground, which allowed others to jump from a grassy bank onto the seesaw. This was not accepted.

- The local council checked the playground twice every week and had the power to right any faults immediately.

- It took six years for the case to reach court.

Judgment:

- The boy's action of jumping onto the seesaw was deemed to be sudden and unexpected, and therefore unforeseeable.

- The local authority was not deemed to be responsible for looking after the boy once the day's voluntary activity had ended. Neither was the authority held to have a legal obligation to provide supervision outside the boundaries and hours of the local centre.

- The woman's offer to join the boy on the seesaw was voluntary and, due to the sudden and unexpected action of the second boy, was not negligent.

- The judge criticised the failure to write a detailed report at the time of the incident.

- The appeal supported the judge's decision in the first instance that no negligence was evident.

Issues to consider:

- It is important to record a contemporaneous report at the time of significant injury so that detail is not forgotten over time.

- Parents should be informed of when and where groups will be received and dismissed, and where responsibility for the children is taken from, and handed back to, the parents.

Case 11

Activity: Rock climbing
Age: Adult
Principle: Educating novices on their own safety

GRAHAM v NEWCASTLE CITY COUNCIL
Newcastle County Court, 2000
Zurich Municipal *Court Circular*, July 2000

Summary:

- A novice climber lost his grip and fell from a climbing wall in the first of a 10-session course for beginners. His feet were between 1.5 and 2 m above the ground at the time of falling.

- The council's guidelines advised beginners not to climb above head height until they had gained confidence over a number of visits.

- Two experienced instructors were supervising 10 novices. It was reported that the course was well planned.

- The novice climber sustained a stress fracture to the spine. The floor was made of shock-absorbing material and was said to be the best available.

Judgment:

- It was held that the claimant, as an adult, could make his own decisions. It was acceptable to allow him to climb to this height.

- The ratio of supervisors to novices was deemed to be good. Even one-to-one supervision would not have prevented the accident.

- It was judged that a safety mat could have presented additional hazards, such as a climber sustaining a sprained ankle by landing on its edge.

- Judgment was made for the defendant – the council. It was claimed that very prescriptive instructions were required for novices, but this argument was dismissed.

Issues to consider:

- The judgment may have been different if a minor had been involved, as they are deemed to be less able to make their own decisions, especially in a school situation.

- Very prescriptive instructions would not be required for young novices, providing they have been involved in, and educated in, the considerations for their own safety.

- Good practice with pupils at school involves appropriate experience of developing progression and competency.

Case 12

Activity: Rugby
Age: Secondary
Principle: Teachers' roles and involvement in games

AFFUTU-NARTAY v CLARK and ANOTHER
Queen's Bench Division, 1994
82 NJ 61 (Transcript: Association)
Lexis

Summary:

- A 15-year-old pupil, playing rugby during a physical education lesson, was injured in a tackle and became temporarily paraplegic. Some recovery occurred but the pupil still suffers back pain.

- The teacher in charge was supervising, officiating, coaching and participating in the game. He was described as being 'fit and strong; a very experienced rugby footballer and, of course, far faster, fitter and stronger than the boys of 15 who were under his supervision'.

- During the game, the pupil gathered the ball and received a high tackle at speed by the teacher, who grasped the pupil's shirt collar and swung him off the ground. The pupil landed heavily on his back, fell temporarily unconscious and lost the feeling in his legs.

Judgment:

- The teacher was found to be negligent and the LEA vicariously liable. The teacher should not have tackled the pupil at all.

- According to Judge Hodgson, the teacher was held to be:

  enjoying the game and more anxious than he should have been to assist his own team to victory...he momentarily forgot that he was playing with young school boys and perpetrated on the plaintiff a tackle which he should never have done. That sort of thing is so likely to happen in the heat of the moment that...in rugby football, which is about the only game played in this country where there is actual upper body contact between players as a lawful and deliberate part of the game, it is wrong and a breach of the duty of care owed to the school boys, for a master taking part in the game to have any intentional physical contact with the boy.

- This decision was compounded by the further comment:

  That does not mean that he (the teacher) cannot play an active part in the game, but the object should not be to support one side or the other but to keep the game moving and the ball moving and to demonstrate the skills of the game, which he has in so much more marked a degree than the boys with whom he is playing.

Issues to consider:

- The judgment clearly states that the teacher was not at fault by placing himself in a team of pupils. This would be wholly acceptable in order to simply demonstrate passive and non-contact skills.

- The mistake was to become involved in physical contact because it was foreseeable that it could cause injury. It was also foreseeable that the responsible adult may forget in the excitement of the game and perform a dangerous, high tackle. The risk of injury in such circumstances is deemed to be unacceptably high. The judgment held the teacher to be negligent for tackling a pupil at all.

- The judgment has caused schools to carefully reflect on the wisdom of *staff versus pupils* matches in any activity. The issues raised by the judgment about adults being faster, fitter, more experienced and often heavier makes a mismatch very obvious in any sport where physical contact at a speed is even a possibility, let alone part of the game.

Case 13

Activity: Rugby
Age: Secondary
Principle: Inadequate officiating of games

SMOLDEN v WHITWORTH
Court of Appeal, 1996
The Times, **23 April 1996**
Lexis

Summary:

- A player was paralysed from the shoulders down when a scrum collapsed during an under-19s rugby game.

- Negligence was alleged against the referee for failing to enforce the laws of the game in order to ensure the safety of the players, thereby exposing them to unnecessary risk.

Judgment:

- The referee was found to be liable in the first instance, which was then confirmed at appeal.

- This judgment does not change the law as it stands. Referees have a duty of care towards players.

- However, it highlights existing, potential liabilities for head teachers and teachers.

- It has long been held that sports officials, including teachers, may be liable if they fail to carry out their duties to control a game within the rules of the sport. The *appeal court* rejected the view that liability only exists if the referee shows reckless disregard for the player's safety. Lord Justice Bingham said, 'The level of care which is required of a referee is inextricably linked to the circumstances under which a game occurs and this threshold is a high one'.

- The referee failed to apply two rules that are essential to safe play – the drive (crouch – touch – pause – engage: CTPE) and shoulder/hip positions. He also allowed more than 30 collapsed scrums without giving a penalty. The standard fell below that expected of a reasonably competent referee.

- The standard of care required is an objective one, relating to the foreseeable risk to participants and not to the subjective skill of the referee.

- It allocates responsibility for sports injuries suffered by young people, as the official is the last person able to prevent foreseeable harm to the players.

Issues to consider:

- The judge's decision affects those who are responsible for the control of sport activities in which others are likely to be injured. Referees and umpires who spot something incorrect must instruct and correct (as well as referee) as they have both a duty of care and a duty of control. This means that referees in school rugby matches are expected to assume much more responsibility for the welfare of the players than referees in matches at senior level. This is due to the differences between teams in levels of skill, fitness and maturity.

- Schools have a duty of care to ensure that competent adults teach, supervise and officiate sport activities, whether as part of curricular or extra-curricular activity.

- Curricular and voluntary sport must be properly authorised and organised by the school.

- The judgment confirms the responsibility of teachers or managers of school teams (who are probably not refereeing) to intervene and consult referees, or even abandon matches, if they believe that serious injury is foreseeable due to a lack of stringent officiating.

- Teachers must be absolutely clear about when they are working within their contracts and when separate, third party insurance is necessary.

Case 14

Activity: Rugby
Age: Adult
Principle: Inadequate supervision

VOWLES _v_ EVANS and OTHERS (WELSH RUGBY FOOTBALL UNION)
High Court, London, 2002
Daily Mail, 14 December 2002

Summary:

- A player was paralysed after a scrum collapsed in a rugby match.

- An inexperienced front row forward had been substituted for an injured, experienced prop, which led to repeated scrum collapses.

- The poor weather conditions affected footing.

- The referee allowed contested scrums to continue as normal.

- The Welsh Rugby Football Union (WRFU) accepted vicarious responsibility for the official's failure to opt for uncontested scrums (which present less risk of crush injuries) in the light of the particular circumstances.

Judgment:

- The judgment was in support of the claim but an appeal may yet be made.

- The case hinged on whether the referee should have insisted on uncontested scrums after an inexperienced front row forward was substituted for an experienced player.

- Justice Morland said, 'It is just and reasonable that the law should impose upon an amateur referee of an amateur rugby match a duty of care towards the players'.

Issues to consider:

- Adult players accept the risk of injury by choosing to participate within the rules and spirit of the game. However, existing case law supports the principle that such acceptance of risk does not apply to issues outside the said rules and spirit, particularly at school level.

- This case was the first in which an amateur referee in any sport had been held responsible for injuries in an adult game. (The _Smolden_ judgment on page 84 was specific to young people.)

- The judgment makes sports governing bodies responsible for a duty of care on the field. This may lead to significant changes in the officiating requirements for national governing bodies.

- The decision does not alter existing standards and expectations for teachers officiating in school matches, which are described in further detail in the _Smolden_ summary (Case 13, page 84).

Case 15

Activity: Scuba diving
Age: Adult
Principle: Inadequate tuition

PERCIVAL v CORPORATION OF LEICESTER
Leicester Assizes, 1962
Lexis

Summary:

- An off-duty fireman drowned in a gravel pit while practising aqua lung swimming.

- His widow alleged negligence based on inadequate instruction, the deceased being allowed to swim without a safety line, the lack of a requirement permit to practise sufficiently and the provision of defective equipment.

- Evidence suggested that practices were infrequent, with a nine-month break between phases of training.

- The fireman had dived into the gravel pit before and had all the necessary equipment.

- The dive was deemed to be progressing satisfactorily. However, the fireman suddenly appeared at the surface calling for help, having torn off his mask. The court was unable to establish the cause of the incident, except that he was not wearing a nose clip when rescued and had not used a safety line.

- Others in the group confirmed that all the essential safety issues had been adequately covered.

Judgment:

- It was held that the trainee divers had been instructed properly and efficiently. It was also judged that people do not forget what they have been taught, despite a lay-off (of nine months in this case). The adult trainees would have been expected to take things slowly when diving for the first time in nine months.

- It was determined that, had the diver worn a safety line, it would have saved his life. It was also established that the need to use a safety line was fully understood by the group. The deceased, however, had chosen not to follow these set procedures.

- The claim was dismissed.

Issues to consider:

- It is essential to check that procedures are followed and essential equipment is used. Even when groups are beginning to work independently, such requirements should be monitored and action taken if it is noticed that individuals make omissions.

- Following a gap between practices or a lengthy absence from activity, participants should be reminded to take things easy and revise the essential points before putting them into practice.

Case 16

Activity: Self-defence
Age: Adult
Principle: Teacher expertise

Summary:

- The claimant injured her shoulder when attending a self-defence course devised by her employers, South Glamorgan Health Authority, in response to increased violent behaviour by mentally disturbed patients.

- The claimant participated in a demonstration with the course instructor on a technique to release oneself from a floor choke. The claimant said that she sat astride the instructor to participate, expecting a gentle demonstration of how to remove an aggressor's hands from around the neck. She alleged that the instructor performed an unexpected, different movement in a more aggressive manner than she had anticipated. She fell onto her side with her arm behind her, thus injuring her shoulder. It was claimed that it was a foreseeable injury.

- The instructor claimed to have followed the technique shown on video and as she had been trained. She alleged that the claimant had not been listening, did not roll and thus fell awkwardly. The defence claimed that the risk was of no significance if instructions were followed.

Judgment:

- The judge commended the principle of providing the course.

- The judge accepted the instructor's description of events, finding it 'inconceivable that she would suddenly employ a wholly new technique'.

- The judge also accepted that the claimant had not followed the instructions given.

- He concluded that there was a foreseeable significant risk to the activity, which required some practice in preparatory rolling. He acknowledged that the skill needed introducing gently and that the instructors had not been taught how to teach, thus being inadequately prepared for what they had responsibility for. The accident could have been avoided.

Analysis of Case Law to Identify Issues for School Staff, Coaches and Volunteers

Issues to consider:

- This judgment has implications for those teaching physical education. They must:
  - be fully taught or prepared
  - have a level of expertise in all the activities they are required to teach
  - provide necessary progressive practices
  - check that pupils understand and have a reasonable knowledge of the activity
  - avoid situations in which injury is foreseeable.

- Pupils should be fully aware of what they need to do when participating in a demonstration or performing a skill.

- Adults should think carefully before demonstrating by using pupils in competition against themselves.

Case 17

Activity: Swimming
Age: Primary
Principle: Inadequate supervision

BURKE v CARDIFF CITY COUNCIL
Court of Appeal, 1986
Transcript: Association
Lexis

Summary:

- A 10-year-old boy went to the city's Olympic-sized swimming pool with two friends.

- There were approximately 250 people in the pool, around 40 of whom were in the deep end.

- The claimant was not a strong swimmer. He could swim approximately 25 m, while his friends were stronger swimmers.

- At the deep end (of approximately 4.5 m) there were a number of diving boards, including a low springboard approximately 3 m from the side of the pool.

- On arrival, the three boys went straight to the deep end and dived in from the springboard. The claimant surfaced, struggled and panicked. His friends tried to rescue him.

- The claimant reached the side and then sank. His friends tried to attract the lifeguard's attention. However, he was approximately 15 m away, leaning on a railing and looking in the opposite direction, so the friends were not immediately successful at attracting his attention. Eventually, the lifeguard became aware of the situation and rescued the claimant.

- The lifeguard applied artificial respiration and an ambulance was called. The claimant was unconscious when removed from the building. He suffered severe brain damage and remains in an insensitive state.

- No evidence emerged regarding whether or not the level of lifeguard supervision was appropriate.

Judgment:

- In the first instance, the judge held that the level of poolside supervision was inadequate and that the time it took to attract the lifeguard's attention constituted a breach of duty of care.

- The lifeguard's level of awareness was also considered to be inadequate.

- At appeal, it was confirmed that:

    A proper standard of surveillance would have alerted the guard to that fact that [the claimant was in difficulty] and in all probability, he would have been able to rescue the child before he ever became submerged. If this child had been rescued on the surface of the water, no brain damage would have ensued.

- Negligence was confirmed.

Issues to consider:

- Prior to a visit to a swimming pool, levels of poolside supervision need to be determined through a risk assessment, according to the specific circumstances at the pool.

- Lifeguards should constantly scan all areas of the swimming pool in order to remain alert to what is happening. Distractions, such as watching particular groups for extended periods of time, should be avoided.

- While this incident occurred during an open session at a public pool, attracting an adult's attention to an incident in a school situation should be explicit and within normal operating procedures.

Case 18

Activity: Swimming
Age: Primary
Principle: Inadequate tuition

JONES v CHESHIRE COUNTY COUNCIL
Manchester County Court, 1997

Summary:

- The claimant, a nine-year-old girl, was injured during a 30-minute swimming lesson, which involved 32 children in Year 4.

- The pool was a learner pool, approximately 12 m x 6 m in area. The depth at the shallow end was 0.7 m and, at the deep end, 1 m. The pool had a gently sloping, tiled bottom.

- The lesson was taken by the class teacher, a very experienced swimming instructor at the school. The child was a competent swimmer and confident in the water. It was the class' final swimming lesson of the summer term.

- The LEA guidelines recommended a ratio of one teacher to 20 pupils for swimming. During the lesson, the teacher operated a pairing system of one child in the water with one sitting out on the side. The pupils swapped at frequent intervals. This resulted in a maximum of 16 pupils in the water at any one time.

- At the end of the swimming lesson, the teacher allowed all the children to enter the water for a couple of minutes of *free activity*. The injured pupil chose to work with a partner in the shallowest water. They took it in turns to dive and swim underwater between each other's straddled legs. The pupil suffered serious injuries to her teeth when her mouth struck the bottom of the pool.

- The teacher stated that the children had not been given permission to dive between each other's legs. The injured child said that this skill had been taught to the class at some stage and that other children were practising the same activity during the period of free activity.

- The teacher had not noticed the underwater diving and swimming activity taking place.

Judgment:

- The teacher was found to be negligent. The activity was deemed to be inherently hazardous, unless the children had been properly instructed by the teacher on how to do it safely in shallow water. There should also have been suitable reminders in subsequent swimming lessons during which this particular activity took place. This had not happened.

- It was held that 32 children in the water at one time was in excess of local authority guidelines and was greater than the number the teacher might reasonably have been capable of supervising in a safe manner.

Issues to consider:

- Locally defined *adult to pupil* ratios for swimming instruction should be noted and observed.

- Underwater swimming/diving in shallow water should be properly taught. Pupils should be instructed to lead with their hands as they approach the bottom of the pool.

- Risk management should be undertaken with pupils, so that they are aware of any hazards and the ways in which these may be properly avoided. Risks include striking the bottom of the pool, striking a side wall of the pool and closing their eyes underwater.

- Choosing an activity to end the lesson, which is based on the skills practised during the lesson, is more focused and predictable than *free activity*.

Case 19

Activity: Swimming
Age: Secondary
Principle: Extent of adequate supervision

CLARKE v BETHNEL GREEN BOROUGH COUNCIL
King's Bench Division, 1939
2 All ER 54
Lexis

Summary:

- The claimant was injured while attending a swimming session at a local council swimming pool.

- She was standing on the diving board preparing to dive when another child, underneath the board, reached up and hung onto it. The child then let go of the board, throwing the claimant against the poolside and causing injury.

- The claimant alleged inadequate supervision and control.

Judgment:

- The claim was dismissed. The judge acknowledged that supervision was needed and that, with one person on the poolside, this was sufficient.

- The poolside supervisor was not deemed to be negligent as she was providing general supervision and, according to Judge Oliver, 'was not bound to see a performance which affected two out of 50'.

Issues to consider:

- It is important to remember that this case took place in 1939. Judgment is likely to be different today, due to the expectation for specific risk assessments to determine staffing levels according to the size and design of the pool, the numbers involved and the activities going on.

- Those responsible for pupils are expected to inform the pupils about their own safety, to draw attention to hazardous acts, and to more securely supervise areas of greater hazard.

Case 20

Activity: Trampolining
Age: Adult
Principle: Working within or outside contracts

STENNER v TAFF-ELY BOROUGH COUNCIL
Court of Appeal, 1987
Transcript: Association
Lexis

Summary:

- A qualified gymnastics coach employed by the Borough Council was given permission by the leisure centre manager to use the facility on an occasion when it was not open to the public. He wanted to do some gymnastic coaching with his children and an adult friend.

- They used a trampoline and a trampette. However, the adult friend had never used such equipment before and, as a result, he was left paraplegic and permanently paralysed. The coach was not in close attendance at the time of the injury.

- The injured adult sued the Borough Council for vicarious liability for the negligence.

- The gymnastics coach was not separately insured.

Judgment:

- The claim was supported in the first instance but reversed at appeal.

- The issue focused on whether or not the gymnastics coach was working in the course of his employment. He had permission to use the facility to coach gymnastics, even though the centre was closed to the public at the time and he was not being paid.

- The *appeal court* held that the local authority was not liable merely because the gymnastics coach was acting with the authority's knowledge, acquaintance or permission. Lord Justice Balcombe said, 'A master is not responsible for the negligence of his servant while engaged in doing something which he is permitted to do for his own purposes but not employed to do for his master. I am liable only for what I employ my servant to do for me, not for what I allow him to do for himself'.

- It was held that the gymnastics coach was engaged in a private family affair and was not acting in the course of his employment.

- It was acknowledged that the coach was negligent.

Issues to consider:

- Due to the wide range of additional activities in which school staff often become involved, it is essential for members of staff to clarify whether they are working within the course of employment, or participating in a private capacity in which they possibly have permission to use particular facilities. Such situations may include outdoor activities, trips, or holiday sports coaching courses held on the school grounds. Working within the course of one's employment involves:
  - the head teacher's knowledge and approval of the event and confirmation that the event is official
  - possible school governing body approval for the event, which is usually communicated through the head teacher.

- School staff should ensure that the head teacher is fully aware of all planned activities in and out of curriculum time so that any possible instances of working outside the conditions of employment are clarified.

- School staff involved in sports activities that are not directly associated with the school (eg regional sports associations, delivering national governing body awards or working with independent groups) must be covered by appropriate third party liability insurance. According to the circumstances, they should check whether this is provided by:
  - the LEA/governors as an employer
  - the national governing body of sport
  - independent arrangements.

- It is important to provide appropriate progressive activities, cater for the individual's ability or needs, and be in a position of close supervision when a task new to a person is first attempted. One feature referred to by the *appeal court*, but not central to its deliberations, was the negligence of the gymnastics coach in not adhering to these guidelines.

- Members of staff or coaches are vulnerable if they do not have insurance against third party liability.

5.2 CASES OF NEGLIGENCE RELATING TO PEOPLE: PUPILS AND PARTICIPANTS

Case 21

Activity: Athletics (indoors)
Age: Adult
Principle: Involving participants in their own safety and the level of duty of care in a disabled participant context

MORREL v OWEN and OTHERS
Queen's Bench Division, 1993
The Times, **14 December 1993**
Lexis

Summary:

- A disabled archer attended a national governing body training weekend for competent performers, which involved archery and discus events: both sharing a sports hall.

- The organisers had arranged similar events that shared facilities on previous occasions, but the claimant was attending her first and claimed to be unaware that the other group was throwing discuses.

- The discus group threw the distance of a few metres towards the dividing net, while the archers worked across the hall. The discuses caused the dividing net to balloon into the archery area and thus space was limited for the archers.

- The archers had to pass through the end of the dividing net and along the discus area in order to leave the hall. This was not policed for safety purposes.

- The wheelchair user, on returning to the archery side of the net after re-entering the hall, had to wait for the archery group to finish shooting. While waiting, she was hit on the head by a discus that ballooned the dividing net into the archery area. The discus thrower and coaches claimed to have told the claimant to move further into the crowded archery area to avoid being hit.

- The supervising coaches had left safety responsibility to the experienced participants. There had not been a collective safety discussion or induction. The groups had not been brought together to explain what each group was doing and the possible implications of this.

- The claimant, along with other archers, had not noticed any activity in the other part of the hall when they passed through.

- The claimant alleged negligence against the organisers and the discus thrower for the injuries she sustained.

Judgment:

- The claim was upheld because, 'on the balance of probabilities, the organisers neglected to exercise the care which the law required'.

- Justice Mitchell held that, 'in terms of safety precautions and the need for workable and explicable procedures, the attitude of the coaches (that the participants were experienced and thus no safety instruction was necessary) is absurd'.

- It was also held 'more than probable that the attitude of both the discus coaches and athletes was that the archers at, or near, the gap should immediately fall in with any request or requirement regardless of the archers' circumstances and regardless of the circumstances then prevailing on the archery side of the net. The discus throwers, in short, afforded themselves priority'.

- Emphasis was given to the circumstances that 'you cannot simply apply normal standards to disabled sports activities. The disabled are not always ambulant. In any event, movement can take longer and there will always be a range of disabilities involved'.

- A counter claim for contributory negligence was dismissed. This was on the grounds that it had not been established that the injured archer had been negligent as, 'with a clear understanding of the risk, she carelessly ignored them'.

Issues to consider:

- Pupils should be fully appraised of the safety issues relating to activities in which they are involved. Furthermore, they should be involved in their own safety, at a level commensurate with their age, through a programme of safety education.

- Multi-activity arrangement in a single facility requires effective management with clear areas of work, *run-off* space and clear arrangements for action should anyone need to move into another working area for any reason.

- Depending on the disabilities and activities involved, it may be necessary to allow more time for less able participants to complete particular tasks. This may have subsequent safety and management implications.

Case 22

Activity: Football
Age: Adult
Principle: Duty of care owed to other players

> **CONDON v BASI**
> **Court of Appeal, 1985**
> **(1985) 2 All ER 453, (1985) 1 WLR 866 CLJ 371**
> **Lexis**

Summary:

- During a football match, a player about to be challenged pushed the ball away. The opponent then performed a late sliding tackle from 3–4 m away. His studs were reported to be showing.

- Contact was made with the claimant's leg approximately 25 cm above the ground, causing a broken leg.

- The offender was sent off.

Judgment:

- A guilty of negligence verdict was passed and then confirmed at appeal.

- At the time of the case, Lord Donaldson (Master of the Rolls) found that: 'there is no authority as to what is the standard of care which governs the conduct of players in competitive sports generally...whose rules and general background contemplate that there will be physical contact between the players...this is somewhat surprising but appears to be correct'.

- The basis for the decision was that 'the defendant failed to exercise that duty of care which was appropriate in all the circumstances, or that he acted in a way to which the plaintiff cannot be expected to have consented. In either event, there is liability...thus establishing a duty of care between players against causing foreseeable dangers'.

- It was held that 'there was an obvious breach of duty of care...of serious foul play which showed a reckless disregard...and which fell far below the standards which might reasonably be expected in anyone pursuing the game'.

Issues to consider:

- Staff/managers must insist that pupils play within the rules and culture of the game. Reckless play may result in legal action, in which the adult may be implicated as the person responsible for the pupils' actions.

- Responsible adults must educate pupils about the duty of care pupils owe their fellow players.

Case 23

Activity: Football
Age: Adult
Principle: Duty of care owed to other players

PARRY v McGUCKIN
Queen's Bench Division, 1990
IV Gilbert
Lexis

Summary:

- A player received a serious, permanent knee injury during a late, high tackle from behind in a football match with significant local rivalry.

- There were mixed reports. The defendant denied contact, but called witnesses who described it as misadventure in a perfectly proper tackle, which involved contact. The claimant alleged that the defendant had performed a dangerous and reckless tackle.

- Justice Ward acknowledged a risk of injury in football but said:

  The mere fact that somebody receives injury in the course of a tackle does not entitle him to claim damages from the man tackling him and causing injury. Even if there is mismanagement on the part of the tackler, which may well result from the speed at which the game must normally be played, that is not negligence at common law...but if a tackle is reckless and dangerous then it follows that it is negligence.

Judgment:

- The defendant was held to be negligent. Justice Ward rejected his claim of no contact because it was completely different to all the other testimonies and said, 'His attempt to distance himself from any physical contact with the plaintiff can only indicate, in my opinion, a guilty conscience on his part. I am satisfied that, on the balance of probabilities,...it was unfair, dangerous and wholly unacceptable'.

- Careful attention was given to the referee's evidence. No criticism was made of him or his refereeing ability.

- Reference was made to the fact that the incident occurred before the *Condon v Basi* decision in 1985, even though it came to court later and was thus at a time when 'those who took part in sports involving physical contact hardly seem to have realised that it was open to them to bring action for damages. It was not uncommon...to accept even unlawful behaviour as part of the risks inevitably run by anybody taking part'.

Issues to consider:

- Staff should ensure that pupils play within the rules and culture of the game.

- Those officiating in matches must apply the laws strictly, in order to avoid possible challenges of negligence themselves. Staff should carefully organise and supervise games and lessons, and must be strict and vigilant when refereeing.

Case 24

Activity: Football
Age: Adult
Principle: Reckless play

ELLIOT v SAUNDERS and ANOTHER
Queen's Bench Division, 1994
Transcript: Chilton Vint
Lexis

Summary:

- A claim was made by a professional footballer for damages due to personal injury and loss suffered as a result of a tackle by the first defendant.

- The claimant argued that the defendant had deliberately committed a foul by going for him instead of the ball. This constituted a deliberate or reckless breach of the rules and a failure to exercise the necessary duty of care.

- It was held that, 'if the injury was caused by another player acting in a wholly unacceptable manner, for example, by intending to cause injury, or being reckless, not caring whether or not injury was caused, then surely it is right that the injured person should be able to claim compensation'.

- The judge also said:

  Football is a game necessarily involving strong physical contact...sometimes played at a very fast speed...involving quick decisions as to how to react to the situation immediately confronting them. Therefore, an error of judgement or a mistake will not always mean that the player has failed to exercise the duty of care appropriate in the circumstances.

- Both players leapt into the tackle with both feet off the ground. The claimant argued that the defendant jumped at him rather than at the ball in a reckless manner, but without deliberate intent to cause harm.

- The defendant argued that, had he kept his feet on the ground and not jumped, he would have been injured by the claimant's actions. He claimed that he jumped to avoid injury and not to cause it. It was, he argued, an instinctive reaction.

- Photographic, video and expert witness opinion did not provide conclusive evidence.

- The referee had awarded a penalty to the defendant on account of the claimant's dangerous play when jumping into the tackle. The claimant was then injured by the other's evasive action. The Football Association (The FA) adjudicator supported the referee's actions.

Judgment:

- The judge directly linked this case with the *Condon v Basi* case (page 100).

- The judge said, 'Unless, and until, video is introduced by the governing body of a sport, as an aid to the referee or umpire, his decision on the field must be final as regards what happens during the game'.

- The judge fully accepted the evidence given, along with the decisions of the referee and linesman, who both felt that the claimant's tackle was dangerous and that he was injured by the evasive (though not reckless) action of the defendant.

- The claim was rejected. The judge held that the claimant failed to prove that the defendant jumped on or at him. The defendant was not in breach of the duty of care he owed the claimant.

Issues to consider:

- Players in contact sports are sometimes accidentally injured.

- It should be insisted that all players perform within the rules and spirit of the game. Good techniques should be reinforced with players.

- Referees should referee vigilantly and their decision should be final.

- Players should be reminded that, in football, staying on one's feet rather than sliding into a tackle, is more likely to lead to keeping control of the ball after the tackle is completed.

Case 25

Activity: Football
Age: Adult
Principle: The duty owed to other players

McCORD *v* SWANSEA FOOTBALL CLUB
Queen's Bench Division, 1997
Transcript: Smith Burnal
The Times, 11 February 1997
Lexis

Summary:

- The claimant was injured in a tackle by a Swansea player during a football league match.

- The players collided when going for a loose ball.

- The damage to the broken leg was such that it ended the claimant's football career.

- There was no evidence of ill feeling during the game. There was no suggestion of any tendency towards reckless play.

- Both players ran towards a loose ball said to be in favour of the claimant. The defendant used a sliding tackle. The key element in the case was whether or not it was a high tackle.

- The defendant's foot reached the ball a fraction of a second after the claimant's, striking his calf and breaking both bones.

- At the time of the injury, there were no complaints from opponents that the tackle was over the ball.

- The judge watched a video of the game, carefully re-running the relevant section.

- The fourth FA official described the tackle to be 'in the top three worst challenges' he had seen, as it was both late and over the ball. He described it as a 'dreadful tackle, with no attempt to play the ball'.

Judgment:

- The judge said:

  Authority is scarce as to the duty owed in law by one sportsman to another. [The] Condon v Basi [case], 1995, is not dissimilar. The defendant is liable if it is found that he failed to exercise that degree of care which was appropriate...or that he acted in a way to which the plaintiff [claimant] cannot be expected to have consented.

  If the conduct is deliberately intended to injure somebody, or is reckless and in disregard of all safety of others so that it is a departure from standards which might reasonably be expected...then the performer might well be held liable for any injury his act caused.

  A person attending a game or competition takes the risk of any damage caused to him by any act of a participant done in the course of, and for the purpose of, the game or competition (ie within the rules and spirit of the game), not withstanding that such an act may involve an error of judgement or lapse of skill, unless the participant's conduct is such as to evince a reckless disregard of the spectator's safety.

- It was clearly recognised that an error of judgement or a mistake does not always mean that the duty of care was broken.

- A final judgment was made that balanced the claims that the tackle was fair and responsible and that it was late, over the ball and reckless.

- It was held that the tackle had been dangerous and that a misjudgement carried a real risk of serious injury. The defender was guilty of a serious mistake or misjudgement when he tackled so that his foot passed clear over the ball while the players were in *front-on* positions.

- The tackle was described as 'inconsistent with taking reasonable care towards the claimant'. Damages were allowed.

Issues to consider:

- Good techniques should be reinforced with players.

- It should be insisted that all players perform within the rules and spirit of the game.

- Players should be reminded that, in football, staying on one's feet rather than sliding into a tackle is more likely to lead to keeping control of the ball after the tackle is completed.

Case 26

Activity: Football
Age: Adult
Principle: Reckless play

> **WATSON v GRAY**
> **Court of Appeal, 1999**
> **Transcript: Smith Bernal**
> **Lexis**

Summary:

- During a professional football match, the defendant tackled the claimant with such force that he broke the defendant's leg.

- Players, officials and spectators confirmed that the tackle was very late. The player was cautioned for the offence but was not sent off.

- The claimant sought damages for reckless play.

Judgment:

- In the first instance, the judge found the tackle to be negligent but not reckless.

- The judge deemed the tackle to be 'very forceful, high...and late...in the sense that the ball had been pushed on before contact was made...it was fractionally late'.

- The expert evidence of well-known, former professional footballers was not accepted as they sought to 'play down the nature of the challenge'.

- The judge said that 'the defendant's behaviour created a risk of injury which went beyond the accepted risk which is inherent in a game of football...but it had not been reckless'.

- The appeal against the judgment that the tackle was not reckless was dismissed.

Issues to consider:

- Stringent officiating and applying the rules is essential.

- Players remaining on their feet when tackling are less likely to commit offences.

Case 27

Activity: Golf
Age: Secondary
Principle: Behaviour

CUTHBERTSON v MERCHISTON CASTLE SCHOOL
Edinburgh Sheriff Court, April 2000
Zurich Municipal *Court Circular*, September 2001

Summary:

- A school group visiting a golf driving range was supervised by a teacher and golf professional.

- A pupil swinging a club in an attempt to hit a bouncing ball struck a fellow pupil in the face. The injured pupil was practising in a covered bay at the time of the incident.

- It was argued that the staffing level was inadequate and that another member of staff should have been provided.

- It was claimed that, 'unlike local authority schools, resources were not a major concern'.

Judgment:

- The claim was dismissed.

- The judge held that:
  - the standard of care does not depend on the type of institution
  - striking golf balls in a range designed for that purpose is not inherently dangerous
  - there was no reason for the teacher to have anticipated the act of misbehaviour that led to the accident.

Issues to consider:

- Allocating and monitoring appropriate space according to the demands of the activity is essential.

- Adequate supervision is necessary in order to monitor behaviour.

Case 28

Activity: Golf
Age: Adult
Principle: Inadequate control

BREWER v DELO
Queen's Bench Division, 1967
1 Lloyd's Rep 488
Lexis

Summary:

- A golfer was struck in the eye by a golf ball while waiting to play his shot on the sixth fairway.

- The defendant had intended to drive down the eleventh fairway. This was parallel to the sixth and was 30 m wide. It was separated from the sixth by 20 m of rough and some trees that were 4–5 m high.

- The defendant hooked the ball and it bounced, striking the claimant who was 200 m away.

- The claimant alleged that the defendant failed either to observe or take heed of the group on the sixth fairway, which was within range. The claimant also argued that the defendant failed to warn the group.

- The defendant denied the claim, saying it was not foreseeable that his ball would strike the plaintiff. It was, he argued, simply a bad shot. He also relied on the doctrine of *volenti non fit injuria*. This means that those volunteering to take part in the activity accept the risk of injury. He claimed to have shouted 'fore' after playing the shot and said that he had never before hooked a ball onto the adjacent fairway.

- There was no notice at the eleventh tee forewarning players to ensure that the sixth fairway was clear before driving off.

- Another player saw the shot and heard the shout of 'fore'.

Judgment:

- The claim was dismissed. It was held that the defendant 'did nothing which was not normal at this club – no danger was foreseeable'.

Issue to consider:

- Sufficient space, time and forewarning should be allowed according to the abilities of the people involved in an activity. Proficiency and consistency allows for less space than where a player's performance is not usually predictable.

Case 29

Activity: Gymnastics
Age: Secondary
Principle: Peer support

WRIGHT v CHESHIRE COUNTY COUNCIL
Court of Appeal, 1952
2 All ER789, 51 LGR14 WN466
Lexis

Summary:

- A 12-year-old boy injured his elbow while vaulting over a buck during a gymnastics lesson.

- Another boy, who was supporting him, ran off when the bell went for morning break, leaving the claimant to vault without support. He fell and injured himself.

- The pupils had been shown the correct way to support each other by the teacher before being allowed the responsibility.

- The injured pupil claimed that the LEA was vicariously liable due to the teacher's negligence. The pupil alleged that, in not supporting at the buck himself, the teacher had failed to provide a safe environment.

Judgment:

- The LEA was initially held liable but this was reversed at appeal.

- The appeal decision held that:
  - using pupils who were experienced in an activity to support each other was 'regular and recognised practice, not only in this school but in other such schools...and was the recognised practice followed everywhere'
  - the pupils were deemed to be old enough to be reasonably expected to follow the teacher's instructions
  - the pupil who left his supporting role when the bell rang was a cause of the accident
  - this action had never happened before, was contrary to the established routine and was therefore deemed to be unforeseeable.

- It was also held by Lord Justice Birkett that:

  In considering a question of fact, what amounts to reasonable care in any given circumstances depends entirely on the circumstances known to the defendant whose conduct is the subject of the enquiry – everything turns on the nature of the exercise which was being performed at the moment the accident occurred. It was not in any sense a dangerous exercise, but it was, of course, an exercise that needed care in its performance. Here was a boy of twelve years of age who had had seven months' training, and it was clear that he himself did not regard this exercise as one involving any great risk.

Issues to consider:

- Using *regular and approved practice* is a strong defence against a charge of negligence.

- Pupils' ages, previous experience and training, behaviour and responsible attitudes should be considered before they are given the responsibility of supporting each other.

- The organisation and presentation of lessons should be based on *regular and approved practice* – that which has been used widely and over a sufficient period of time, and is therefore shown to be safe if organised properly. *Regular and approved practice* is that which is commonly used nationally and not simply within a limited geographic area or a few other schools.

- Regardless of the nature and level of the programme, responsible adults are expected to only allow activities that reasonably suit the level of ability of each individual involved. The courts generally recognise that no activity is inherently unsafe in itself.

- School staff and coaches should read and follow the advice on supporting and standing by in *Safe Practice in Physical Education and School Sport* (baalpe, 2004)[1].

British Association of Advisers and Lecturers in Physical Education (baalpe). (2004) *Safe Practice in Physical Education and School Sport*. Leeds: Coachwise Solutions. ISBN: 1 902523 68 7.

Analysis of Case Law to Identify Issues for School Staff, Coaches and Volunteers

Case 30

Activity: Gymnastics
Age: Adult
Principle: Level of damages awarded

> **STEWARD v CURRY and ANOTHER**
> **Court of Appeal (Civil Division), 1995**
> **Transcript: John Larking**
> **Lexis**

Summary:

- A mature student, aged 32, was following a specialist diploma course in physical education.

- The student landed on her head as she attempted a backwards dismount from a high beam and suffered a compression fracture to her lower thoracic vertebrae.

- Liability was initially denied but later admitted.

- An appeal sought to reduce the level of damages awarded in the first instance.

Judgment:

- The level of damages awarded was found to be reasonable and the appeal was subsequently dismissed.

Issues to consider:

- A lack of forethought, the omission of reasonably expected actions or the inclusion of unreasonable actions may have lifelong implications for anyone injured.

- Risk assessments, sound observations and appropriate intervention, and reasonable forethought are central to the safe teaching of physical education.

Case 31

Activity: Horse riding
Age: Adult
Principle: Liability of competitors to spectators

WOOLDRIDGE v SUMNER and ANOTHER
Court of Appeal, 1962
2QB43 (1963), 2All ER978 (1962), 3WLR616 (1962)
Lexis

Summary:

- An experienced, skilful competitor was riding a good quality horse in a competition show jumping event at the White City Stadium.

- Benches and tubs were situated approximately half a metre from the edge of the competition arena. Beyond these, a cinder track surrounded the arena.

- A film camera operator, unfamiliar with show jumping events, was standing by the benches. He had been told by a steward to move outside the competition area while the horses were galloping.

- The horse galloped beyond the tubs and benches and the camera operator stepped back. On stepping back, he was knocked down and injured.

- Paying spectators were in the stands, situated a good distance from the arena.

Judgment:

- A claim for occupiers' liability was dismissed and not contested further.

- In the first instance, it was held that the rider brought the horse into a corner of the arena much too fast and it crashed into the line of tubs and benches. If the rider had allowed it to, the horse would have run into the cinder track without harming the spectator. The claimant was allowed damages for negligence.

- This was reversed on appeal. It was held that the rider was not liable because the excessive speed around the corner did not cause the accident. This was deemed to be an error of judgement, not negligence. The *appeal court* also found it an unjustified inference that the horse would have gone onto the cinder track if allowed to do so. They felt that, at the time, the horse rather than the rider was in control.

- Lord Justice Diplock said, 'If, in the course of a game or competition at a moment when he really has not the time to think, a participant by mistake takes a wrong measure, he is not held to be guilty of any negligence'.

- Lord Justice Sellers said, 'Where competitors or players break off from the event or game, or diverge clearly from the rules, there may well be room for liability on them...but whether liability should be placed on a competitor or player who is merely seeking to excel or win, it brings the very purpose on which he is engaged...no court or jury would condemn such endeavour as negligence.'

- It was held that:

  A competitor or player cannot, in the normal case of competition or game, rely on the maxim volenti non fit injuria *(to participate is to consent to injury) in answer to a spectator's claim for there is no liability unless there is negligence...provided the competition or game is being performed within the rules and the requirement of the sport and by a person of adequate skill and competence, the spectator does not expect his safety to be regarded by the participant. If there is a departure from the standards which might reasonably be expected...the performer might well be held liable for any injury his act caused.*

Issues to consider:

- This incident was deemed to be a misjudgement and not negligent.

- If play is within the laws of the game, players will not be held liable for injury to spectators.

- At competitive events where spectators are present, staff should ensure that an adequate distance exists between the spectators and the field of play. This, however, may not be possible in typical school-level matches where spectators may stand on the touchline.

- Staff and officials should adequately ensure that no spectators encroach onto, or beyond, the touchline. Where allowed to encroach, subsequent injury to spectators may cause the official to be held responsible.

Case 32

Activity: Play
Age: Pre-school
Principle: Allurement and adequate supervision of young children

DYER v ILFRACOMBE URBAN DISTRICT COUNCIL
Court of Appeal, 1955
1AllER 581, 1WLR218, 54LGR52, 12JP200
Lexis

Summary:

- The defendant council controlled and managed a playground to which children of all ages were admitted. One of the items provided was a chute with a platform approximately 3.5 m above ground level, a stairway leading up to it and a slide descending on the opposite side of the stairway: a traditional structure.

- The chute 'was of excellent design and sound construction'.

- There were no notices that restricted use by young children unless accompanied.

- An unaccompanied four-year-old fell through the rails on the platform and broke his arm. No other accidents had ever occurred on the chute.

- The boy was reported to have climbed through the rails but it was not known precisely how the injury had occurred.

Judgment:

- It was held that very young children do not perceive danger.

- 'The chute was not safe for the use of an unattended, small child of the [claimant's] age.'

- 'The council must warn of any concealed danger or trap of which the occupier is unaware...but the responsibility for the safety of little children must rest primarily on the parents...it is their duty to see that such little children are not allowed to wander about by themselves.'

Issues to consider:

- Accidents in supervised play are much less frequent than in unsupervised play.

- LEAs provide equipment of reputable and modern design that satisfies European Standards, as will most other providers. If responsible adults are in doubt about safety, for example, during an off-site visit abroad or to a playground where the equipment appears to be very old, a risk assessment of the equipment should be carried out.

- Very young children should be provided with the opportunity to use appropriate equipment.

- The ages and levels of experience of the young people involved should influence the level of supervision.

Case 33

Activity: Rock climbing
Age: Adult
Principle: Responsibility for own safety

YOUNG *v* TAUNTON DEAN BOROUGH COUNCIL
Taunton County Court, 2000
Zurich Municipal *Court Circular*, July 2000

Summary:

- An experienced climber lost her grip on a climbing wall and fell between two and five metres, sustaining a serious ankle fracture.

- The floor had impact-absorbing, 50 mm chip foam matting. Additional weight-absorbent mattresses were available for use when required by climbers.

- The British Mountaineering Council (BMC) recommends that managers do not impose rigid rules: 'The climber's safety lies in exposing him to risk (but not excessive risk), thereby enabling him to develop personal judgement'.

Judgment:

- It was held that a breach of duty had not occurred.

- The defence of *volenti non fit injuria* could have been implemented in that, as an adult, nobody required the claimant to undertake the activity. 'She was not under any supervision and she made her own choices.'

Issues to consider:

- Children should be educated in their own safety and made aware of what they should consider when establishing safe working environments and implementing safe working practices.

- Recommendations on the rigidity of rules require very careful consideration. No advice from national bodies should be interpreted to mean that sensible safety procedures are less relevant to this or any other activity.

Case 34

Activity: Rowing
Age: Secondary
Principle: Pupils acting on behalf of schools

'THELMA' (OWNERS) v UNIVERSITY COLLEGE SCHOOL
Mayor's and City of London Court, 1953
2 Lloyd's Rep 613
Lexis

Summary:

- A school rowing eight collided with a motor launch during a practice row.

- The launch, carrying umpires, was stationary across the river after turning before the start of the race. However, a turning signal had not been sounded as is required by local by-laws.

- Both parties sued for damages to the craft, alleging negligence of the others. The launch owners sued the school and not an individual pupil.

- The governors disclaimed all responsibility, alleging that the damage was caused purely by the negligence of the pupil cox in charge of the rowing eight.

- The cox admitted seeing another boat but did not see the launch turning. He also admitted to being unable to see forward above the heads of the crew.

- The teacher in charge of rowing was a vastly experienced coach and the 16-year-old cox involved had been selected by the head teacher, teacher and president of the boat club. He had been thoroughly trained and knew his duties.

Judgment:

- The races were not simply for pupil entertainment but also benefited the school. Therefore, the cox was acting as an agent of the school governors, using the craft in their interests, and the school was thus liable for his negligence.

- The cox was held to be negligent in failing to look sufficiently well ahead of the rowing eight. He should have seen the stationary launch ahead of him.

- The master of the launch was held liable for not being sufficiently aware of what was happening around him (but to a lesser degree than the cox). The ratio of responsibility for the accident was held to be 25:75 to the master and the cox respectively.

Issues to consider:

- This was the first case in which a pupil was held to be a servant or agent of a school, and where there was deemed to be a vicarious liability by the school for the act of the pupil where no member of staff (ie an employee) was alleged to be negligent.

- The judgment was influenced by the following factors:
  - The governors owned the rowing boat.
  - The craft was used for the school's purpose of training the pupils and entering races.
  - Entering and winning races on behalf of the school enhanced the school's prestige, to the school's benefit.
  - The pupils were using the craft with the permission of the governors as owners.
  - The cox was acting as an agent of the school.

- Pupils acting on behalf of their school or representing their school for the school's benefit may be deemed to be the responsibility of the school if behaving in a negligent manner, whether or not an employee (eg a teacher) is liable during the incident.

5.3 CASES OF NEGLIGENCE RELATING TO CONTEXT: FACILITIES

Case 35

Activity: Athletics
Age: Secondary
Principle: Adequate preparation of facilities

FUTCHER v HERTFORDSHIRE LEA
Luton County Court, 1997

Summary:

- A long jump participant damaged her cruciate ligament when landing during an athletics competition.

- It was alleged that this was caused by landing on a hard crust of sand in the landing area.

- The landing area had been raked but not dug over before the competition began.

Judgment

- The claim was upheld.

Issues to consider:

- Sand in landing areas must be the correct type of sharp sand – not builders' sand.

- Landing areas must be dug – not simply raked – before use, whether for use in lessons or before competition.

- Raking during periods of use must be sufficiently adequate to maintain level, soft, impact-absorbing surfaces for landing.

- There may be times during use when raking becomes insufficient to maintain safe landing areas and digging is therefore required.

- Pupils should be taught to recognise when sandpits have become compacted by impact and should be encouraged to ask for this to be corrected before they jump.

Case 36

Activity: Athletics
Age: Adult
Principle: Parents' races

COMER v THE GOVERNORS OF ST PATRICK'S RC PRIMARY SCHOOL
Court of Appeal, 1997
Smith Bernal
Lexis

Summary:

- During a fathers' race at the local primary school sports day, a parent ran into a wall at the end of the course.

- The adult damaged both wrists and both elbows.

- The mothers and fathers had regularly taken part over a number of years in a race at the end of the children's events.

- There was a low wall parallel with the finish line of the race and a space of approximately 2 m beyond it; spectators usually blocked this.

- The claimant had found it impossible to stop before running through the line of spectators and into the wall on previous occasions. He had mentioned this to the head teacher and complained about the danger to participants and spectators.

- The actual finish line was unclear. Some participants thought it was the wall itself.

Judgment:

- A substantially longer *run-off* was required for children as well as adults. In the first instance it was held that, in such a fun event, the adult claimant was familiar with the layout of the playground, aware of the position of the wall and aware that he must slow down to avoid crashing into it.

- While accepting the hazards of running towards the wall rather than away from it, the judge did not accept that, by arranging the race as they did, the school staff exposed the adult to a foreseeable risk because he was fully aware of the circumstances. The action was dismissed.

- At appeal, it was argued that the school staff owed the claimant a duty to protect him from a 'foreseeable risk of misjudgement in the heat of the race'.

- The race was recognised to be informal and friendly with little emphasis on it being organised by the school. The adults were deemed to be fully aware of the circumstances and had willingly joined in 'a bit of light relaxation'.

- It was held that it would have been apparent to the claimant that 'he was running in the direction of a very obvious brick wall' and that 'it was not reasonably foreseeable that, in these circumstances, any adult in the situation in which this race took place would so run as to expose himself to injury'.

- The finding continued that 'the matter would be different for children, who would no doubt be taking part in races under compulsion' and with less awareness of the hazards.

- The appeal was dismissed.

Issues to consider:

- While adults are deemed to have a greater awareness of their surroundings than young children, it is wise to forewarn volunteers of potential hazards and to organise events so as not to bring these into play.

- Participants taking part in events that are bounded by walls should be advised and taught not to run into barriers at speed. Instead, they should conclude the race earlier and take the speed out of the finish by, for example, touching a line on the floor.

- Risk assessments should even be carried out for *fun* events and the findings should be acted upon.

Case 37

Activity: Badminton
Age: Secondary
Principle: Non-participants in or near play areas

PEACEY v HAVERING LEA
Central London County Court, 2000
Zurich Municipal *Court Circular*, October 2000

Summary:

- A lunchtime supervisor lost an eye when hit by a badminton racket.

- She entered the school hall to instruct a group of pupils who were playing badminton to conclude the activity and put the equipment away.

- She walked across the badminton court, believing that the game had finished. However, she was struck by a player running backwards who was attempting an overhead smash.

- The supervisor had to encroach on the *run-off* area of the court because space was restricted by stacked chairs.

- There was no suggestion that the pupils had been deliberately disobedient. They had simply been engrossed in their match.

- Notices were subsequently put on the entrance doors to instruct people not to enter while games were being played.

Judgment:

- The claim for compensation was dismissed.

- The judge said it was obvious that there was no walkway and that the area was too narrow to cross safely during play.

- What was and was not safe was deemed to be obvious. The judge felt that there was no need to provide guidance regarding this.

- The lunchtime supervisor was judged not to have kept a proper lookout.

Issues to consider:

- Technical guidance is available on *run-off* area dimensions. Where space allows, this should be followed.

- Where space does not allow for a sufficient *run-off* area, pupils should be warned and the situation should be closely monitored.

- Crossing activity areas when games are in progress should be avoided, unless it is certain that the activity has ceased and it is safe for both the players and the person encroaching on the playing area.

- Participants and visitors should be involved in their own safety by developing an awareness of their surroundings.

- If space is particularly limited or designs have inherent risks, such as doors opening onto the work area, warning notices may be advisable.

Case 38

Activity: Cricket
Age: Adult
Principle: Appropriate facility

BOLTON v STONE
House of Lords, 1951
AC 850, 1 A11 ER 1078, 50LGR32
Lexis

Summary:

- During a cricket match, a batsman hit a ball that struck and injured the claimant, who was standing on a road adjacent to the ground.

- There was a protective fence 5 m high at the point the ball was hit out of the ground.

- The distance from the striker to the fence was approximately 70 m and approximately 90 m from where it hit the claimant.

- The ground had been used for cricket for approximately 90 years and on approximately six occasions in 30 years the ball had been hit out of the ground. On these occasions, no one had been injured.

- The claimant alleged negligence against the occupiers of the cricket ground.

Judgment:

- 'For an act to be negligent, there must be not only a reasonable possibility of it happening, but also of injury being caused.'

- In the first instance it was held that, in these particular circumstances, the risk of injury to someone on the highway was so small that the probability could not be reasonably anticipated.

- The case was dismissed. However, the decision was reversed at appeal where it was judged to be a foreseeable risk because it had happened before.

- The appeal was challenged and, in the House of Lords, it was again reversed to the original judgment and the claim was dismissed.

Issues to consider:

- The number of times an incident occurs within a period of time is one indication of the standard of 'reasonable/ordinary/proper care'.

- The lords involved in this decision decided that the few occasions in which this had happened over a period of 30 years did not make the possible injury foreseeable. This contrasts with the very recent *Dickinson v Cornwall County Council* case (Case 52, page 172), in which the defendants were not found to be liable but the fact that the tragedy had happened now made it foreseeable.

- School staff should consider and share examples of *near misses* within the school's mode of practice. This helps to highlight hazards that are in danger of becoming significant risks in terms of the frequency of the event occurring, even though, at the time of the event, no one was actually injured. In these circumstances, a review of risk is worthwhile.

Case 39

Activity: Cricket
Age: Adult
Principle: Negligence and nuisance

MILLER v JACKSON
Court of Appeal, 1977
QB966, 3A11 ER338, 3WLR 20
Lexis

Summary:

- Cricket had been played on a village site since 1905. In 1972, houses were built adjacent to the ground and the Miller family moved in during the cricket season.

- The Millers' garden was only 30 m from the centre of the pitch. A wall of 2 m in height protected the garden. A chain link fence was added, which increased the height to 4-5 m after several balls landed in the garden.

- The club instructed the batsmen 'to try and drive the balls low for four and not to hit them up in the air for six'. The club also offered to supply and fit a safety net over the garden when matches were in progress and to remedy any damage caused. The Millers rejected all offers.

- The Millers claimed damages for negligence and nuisance, and requested an injunction to restrain the club from playing cricket without taking adequate precautions to prevent balls entering the garden.

Judgment:

- In the first instance, the injunction was granted. The club was deemed to be liable because there was a foreseeable risk of injury from the cricket balls. It could not be reasonable to expect the family to live behind shelters.

- At appeal, Lord Denning criticised the local planning committee for allowing houses to be built so close to the ground. He judged that the club had done all that it could to ensure that no balls went into the garden.

- Because the cricket club had been there first and had done all it could to avoid damage to the new properties, Denning adopted the test of whether the use of the ground by the cricket club for playing cricket was a reasonable use of it. He judged it to be so. The interest of the public at large was held to take precedence over the interest of a private individual.

He held that:

The building of the house does not convert the playing of cricket into a nuisance when it was not so before. I would give priority to the right of the cricket club to continue playing cricket on the ground as they have done for the last 70 years. It takes precedence over the right of the newcomer to sit in his garden undisturbed.

- The appeal was allowed.

Issues to consider:

- It is important to allow sufficient space between activity areas and boundaries onto private land.
- Where persons or property are exposed to real risks of being struck by items of sports equipment (eg javelin, discus, football, cricket ball) the need to provide reasonable warning and/or protective fencing should be considered.

Case 40

Activity: Cricket
Age: Adult
Principle: Occupiers' liability

DOUCH v READING BOROUGH COUNCIL
Reading County Court, 2000
Zurich Municipal *Court Circular*, April 2001

Summary:

- The claimant stumbled while running to retrieve a ball in a cricket match.

- He alleged that the fall was caused by two grass-covered humps in the outfield, approximately 10–12 cm high.

- The council acknowledged that the humps had been there for many years.

Judgment:

- The claim was dismissed. The judge described the humps as, 'at most, minor undulations...the sort which are commonplace in many parks, public places and lawns'.

- He added that 'the likelihood of someone falling was very remote indeed, a minimal risk'.

- He also stated:

  The financial implications of having to level out every undulation in every park would be catastrophic. I have played rugby on grounds with all manner of imperfections. The Council cannot be expected to create Twickenham-type surfaces for players of my level. Even if they had carried out risk assessments, they would probably have concluded that there was nothing to be done.

Issues to consider:

- Playing surfaces must be reasonably flat. Slight undulations are acceptable.

- Playing areas must be checked regularly for depressions, undulations and other faults. It must then be decided whether it is reasonable to play fast-moving games involving sudden changes of direction and, possibly, the need to keep a ball under control.

Case 41

Activity: Football
Age: Adult
Principle: Occupiers' Liability Act – responsibilities of those hiring facilities

JONES _v_ NORTHAMPTON BOROUGH COUNCIL and ANOTHER
Court of Appeal (Civil Division), 1990
Transcript: Association
Lexis

Summary:

- The claimant was injured during a five-a-side game of football. His club had hired the indoor games area (a sports hall) at a local leisure centre owned by a borough council.

- An opponent, approaching the claimant to tackle him, slipped on a wet patch on the floor and collided with the claimant, injuring his knee. The wet patch was caused by a leak in the roof.

- The borough council argued that the second defendant (another) – the person actually hiring the pitch and signing the letting agreement – was liable and that his signing of the _Conditions of Hire_ indemnified the local council. The local council argued that the hirer – the second defendant – knew the roof leaked and that the floor was wet. He denied this.

- The claimant sued the council for alleged negligence for not ensuring that the facility was safe for the purpose it was hired and not warning the participants of the presence of water. He later sued the club member who hired the facility (the second defendant – another) for negligence.

- The local council and the second defendant alleged contributory negligence and _volenti non fit injuria_ against the claimant.

- Initially, the council agreed a settlement with the claimant and then sought to recover the costs from the hirer (the second defendant).

- The hirer claimed that the full conditions and responsibilities were not set out on the lettings form but on another, unseen, _Conditions of Hire_ to which his agreed indemnity of the council was given.

Judgment:

- In the first instance, it was held that the local council knew of the leaking roof, wet floor and subsequent risk. The second defendant (the hirer) had been warned of the wet floor and risk, but determined that the competition would go ahead. He therefore knew that the floor was dangerous and held a duty of care to the claimant and other participants. He was in breach of that duty.

- The council was deemed not to be liable because the hirer and players were adults who could make up their own minds about the facility and they had chosen to continue playing.

- Full responsibility was held against the hirer because he had been warned but had been determined to go ahead with the competition without warning the players.

- It was held that 'a signature to a contract is conclusive'. If the hirer signs a lettings form that refers to a more comprehensive list of conditions of hire, he agrees to these whether or not he has seen them, 'by assenting to the contract thus reduced in writing, he represents to the other side that he has made himself acquainted with the contents of that writing and assents to them'.

- At appeal, the judgment that the local council held no contractual liability was overturned. The local council was liable for injury to the claimant. It was also confirmed that the second defendant (the hirer) did owe a duty of care and was in breach of this because he was aware of a danger and neither communicated it nor made alternative arrangements to avoid the danger.

- The Court of Appeal found that the local council could establish a contribution to the settlement by the hirer, but could not be wholly indemnified. It was critical of the way the case had been presented by the claimant's counsel.

Issues to consider:

- The terms of employment should provide staff with insurance against any such claims, when they sign hire or letting agreements within the remit of their work.

- All parties have a duty to inform others of possible dangers that may affect those involved and, where it is within their control, to make alternative arrangements in order to avoid the danger.

- Wet floors present foreseeable risks of injury to participants and must be dealt with before play commences or continues.

- Once responsible adults become aware of anything that threatens the safety of people in their care, action must be taken to remove or reduce the risk to an acceptable level.

Case 42

Activity: Games
Age: Secondary
Principle: Safe environment

RALPH v LONDON CITY COUNCIL
King's Bench Division, 1947
111 JP 246
Lexis

Summary:

- An alternative, indoor physical education lesson took place in the assembly hall due to inclement weather.

- The work area had a partition with glass panels at one end.

- As was common at the time (1947), prescribed physical exercises were followed by a chasing game of tag.

- Free movement was allowed around the whole area.

- The claimant was injured when, in an attempt to avoid capture, he pushed his hand through one of the glass panels.

- Games activities in the hall were usually limited (conditioned) to ensure safety.

Judgment:

- 'It is clear that, without any limitation being put on their movements, the boys taking part in this game would be running madly about the hall, twisting and turning, slipping and sliding.'

- 'Any reasonable and prudent person, leaving regard to the wild nature of the game while it lasted, must (or should) have contemplated that this kind of accident might happen.'

- The LEA, through the teacher in charge, was held to be negligent as the likelihood of such an accident was not anticipated by the teacher.

Issues to consider:

- In older premises, glass should be checked to ensure it complies with current gymnasia standards.

- It is important to take account of identified significant risks in the facility by limiting the area of work or type of activity, or by implementing other appropriate action.

- In 1947, this would have been an acceptable and approved method of warming up. It would not be an acceptable activity today because the standard of care placed on responsible adults is higher than that in 1947.

Case 43

Activity: Games
Age: Adult
Principle: Occupiers' liability (before the Act) – inappropriate facility

GILLMORE _v_ LONDON COUNTY COUNCIL
King's Bench Division, 1938
4 A11 ER 331
Lexis

Summary:

- The claimant joined a physical training class in 1938 and paid a fee.

- The exercises were performed in a hall used for dancing and the floor was highly polished.

- One activity involved hopping on one foot and lunging at others in the group in an effort to make them put their other foot on the ground.

- Each participant was wearing rubber shoes.

- It was alleged that the council, in allowing this activity on a highly polished floor, 'added a danger beyond the usual dangers attending the playing of such a game'.

- The claimant slipped while lunging and was injured. He was judged to be quite athletic and not clumsy.

Judgment:

- It was held that the act of anyone inviting people to pay for some form of physical exercise implies that they have taken reasonable care to ensure that the facility is reasonably safe for the purpose, without implying perfection.

- The claimant was judged to have slipped because of the state of the floor, which was wholly unsuitable.

- A claim of _volenti non fit injuria_ was dismissed. It was held that the claimant trusted those who were in charge and that it never occurred to him that what he was asked to do was dangerous.

- It was held that the claimant was injured because of the added risk of the slippery floor and therefore the council was liable.

Issues to consider:

- It should be ensured, to the best of the responsible adult's knowledge, that the facility is suitable for the activity. The surface, projections and space should be checked.

- Footwear should be checked from time to time so that pupils become educated in the issue of foot and floor traction.

- If a particular situation is judged to be unsafe, the activity, organisation, facility or conditions should be changed in order to make it reasonably safe.

Case 44

Activity: Games
Age: Adult
Principle: Occupiers' liability

MUTIMER *v* MARGATE CORPORATION
Queen's Bench Division, 1956
167 EG 148
Lexis

Summary:

- A man playing a ball game on a public lawn broke his ankle.

- It was alleged that it was the corporation's duty to ensure that the claimant was not exposed to concealed danger. It was argued that this duty was breached because a concealed trap existed due to the lawns being busy with people and the existence of a hole.

- The corporation admitted to being the owners of the lawn but denied that it was a public lawn or recreation ground. Members of the public were admitted to the ground but those who chose to do so took it as they found it. They claimed that the condition of the ground was clear for everyone to see.

- The corporation had filled in holes and re-turfed the area when it took ownership of the land three years previously. Litter was removed and obvious holes filled in daily.

Judgment:

- The claim was dismissed and the action of the corporation was deemed to be reasonable.

Issue to consider:

- Systems should be established to regularly check areas used for playing games in order to ensure reasonable levels of provision for pupils are being maintained. If the areas are prone to holes, stones, broken glass, animal excreta or other problems, alternative areas need to be used.

Case 45

Activity: Games
Age: Adult
Principle: Risk assessments and safe playing surfaces

TAYLOR *v* CORBY BOROUGH COUNCIL
Northampton County Court, 2000
Zurich Municipal *Court Circular*, May 2000

Summary:

- A father and son were playing a ball game on a grassed recreation area. The father's foot went down a hole 10 cm in depth, injuring his leg.

- The hole was partly grassed over.

- Ground maintenance was carried out by a direct labour force that cut the grass 12 times per year. This is typical of many school ground maintenance contracts. The specification required no formal inspections of the playing surface.

- The system of dealing with reported defects was reactive and not based on risk assessments or inspections.

- The area was used extensively and there were no previous instances of injury.

Judgment:

- The judge held that the hole would have been partly visible to anyone looking for it. He decided that the hole had been there for some time without receiving attention.

- The judge believed that the council should have required some positive inspection as, 'if the operator was on the lookout for this sort of hole then, on the balance of probabilities, he would have seen it'.

- The claim for damages was upheld.

Issues to consider:

- Realistic, periodic checks based on a local awareness of the facility are essential. They should be especially rigorous when the facility is used only occasionally or there is an opportunity for damage to occur.

- Risk assessments should be a standard feature.

Case 46

Activity: General
Age: Adult
Principle: Occupiers' liability and the importance of records

GONCALVES v BOURNEMOUTH BOROUGH COUNCIL
Southampton County Court, 2000
Zurich Municipal *Court Circular*, July 2001

Summary:

- The claimant tripped and fell against a door in a sports centre. His arm went through the glass.

- A witness testified that the glass had been cracked, and therefore weakened, for up to three weeks beforehand.

- The defence was based on systems. Duty managers performed routine inspections. A technical team also did inspections. If a crack was found, it was taped over (therefore visible) and replaced within five days. The doors were frequently used by staff and the public, making it unlikely that a crack would have been neglected for long.

- All inspection records had been lost or destroyed. The judge considered this to be 'unfortunate' but not sinister or malicious.

Judgment:

- The evidence claiming that the glass had been broken for at least three weeks was rejected. The claim was dismissed.

- The defendant's (Borough Council) costs were disallowed on the basis that, if the records had been disclosed, a different view may have been taken about pursuing the matter to trial.

- The judge said, 'I shall deprive them of their costs, to send a clear message. They must make sure they preserve documents'.

Issues to consider:

- Risk assessments and other records, such as those relating to maintenance or similar injuries, should be kept for a few years.

- Records form an important part of the defence against allegations of negligence or poor management. This is particularly important with regard to the inspection and maintenance of gymnastic equipment in halls and gymnasia.

- Routines and procedures need to be established and followed in order to identify potential hazards and take appropriate action within an acceptable time period.

- Taping the crack was deemed to be sufficient immediate action in order to limit the weakness in the glass and, in the short term, to draw attention to the fact that something was wrong.

Case 47

Activity: Ice hockey
Age: Primary
Principle: Occupiers' liability (before the Act)

MURRAY v HARRINGAY ARENA LTD
Court of Appeal, 1951
2KB 529, 2 A11 ER 320, WN356
Lexis

Summary:

- A six-year-old claimant was taken by his parents to watch an ice hockey match. They sat in the front row at the side of the rink.

- During the match, the boy was hit in the eye by the puck.

- On behalf of the claimant, it was alleged that a breach had occurred in the implied contract that the arena was 'as safe as care and skill could make it'.

- There was no protection provided beyond a wooden barrier approximately 1 m high at the sides of the rink. Netting approximately 2 m high was provided behind the goals.

- The puck went over the barrier at the side on a number of occasions.

- There had been no evidence of a serious accident happening before this.

Judgment:

- It was held in the first instance that 'the risk of the puck going over the side was not an unusual danger'. There was no negligence, no breach of implied contract and no failure to take ordinary precautions. The claimant voluntarily undertook the risk of accident. It should be noted that this took place in 1951.

- This was upheld at appeal. 'The implied term is not that the occupiers shall guard against every known risk. There are some dangers which every reasonable spectator foresees and of which he takes the risk – the injury sustained by the boy resulted from a danger incident to the game of which spectators took the risk'.

Issues to consider:

- Standards and expectations have changed since 1951, as shown by the provision of spectator protection at modern rinks.

- Spectators still need to accept the risk of injury but not for issues as foreseeable as this.

- When organising spectator events, current guidelines for specific sports (eg athletics) should be followed. Where guidelines are not provided, experience and common sense should be used to determine a safe distance between the court/pitch and the spectators, according to the demands of the game.

Case 48

Activity: Play
Age: Primary
Principle: Occupiers' liability (before the Act)

ELLIS *v* FULHAM BOROUGH COUNCIL
King's Bench Division, 1937
1 ALL ER 698
Lexis

Summary:

- A nine-year-old boy cut his foot on a piece of glass hidden in sand that had silted in a public paddling pool.

- As the pool was a public provision by the council, to which the boy's parent was a rate payer, the boy was deemed to be an invitee by the council and thus owed a higher duty of care than the general public.

- It was alleged that the pool was clearly designed for young children who would remove their shoes and socks to paddle. The council should have realised this and provided supervision or more adequate maintenance. Otherwise, the pool could become a trap (a hidden hazard) leading to injury.

- The council claimed that no duty of care was owed, other than to avoid anything in the nature of a trap. Instructions were issued to council staff to clean the pool but whether or not this was done was not checked.

Judgment:

- It was held that 'there was a hidden danger of which the council ought to have known and would have known if its servants had done their duty. Reasonable care is not limited to the mere provision of the pool and...must extend...to its general management'.

- It was also held that the accident could have been prevented with proper supervision to ensure that the pool was regularly checked. This goes beyond giving instructions for the task to be done.

- The failure to carry out the instructions was seen to be negligent on the part of the council's employees. 'Reasonable care was not given to the child whom the council, through its provision, had invited to use the facility.'

Issues to consider:

- Anyone given a task must ensure that it is carried out or that failure to do so is reported.

- Staff should recognise that management involves monitoring and not simply delegation.

- The provision of a facility, with or without a charge being made, entails the responsibility of ensuring that it is adequately maintained and supervised if others are to use it.

Case 49

Activity: Play area
Age: Primary
Principle: Occupiers' liability (before the Act)

SUTTON v BOOTLE CORPORATION
Court of Appeal, 1946
KB359, 1ALL ER 92, 45 LGR 160, 177 LT 168
Lexis

Summary:

- A nine-year-old child was playing on a swing in a public park.

- The top joint of one of the child's fingers was amputated when it was caught between the unguarded lug and socket of a checking device that prevented the swing from going too far.

- The defect could easily have been remedied but there was no previous evidence of similar injuries and the corporation was unaware of the danger.

Judgment:

- In the first instance the corporation was held liable for the injury, even though it was 'bound to do no more than warn of dangers known' to it.

- At appeal, it was determined that the corporation 'had neither knowledge nor suspicion that this danger was present'. No legal liability was incurred and the appeal dismissed liability for the injury.

Issues to consider:

- Current standards of play equipment are extremely high. This type of injury is unlikely to occur today.

- Regular maintenance checks on equipment are now required under the Provision and Use of Work Equipment Regulations 1992. This has implications for the annual inspection of gymnastic equipment. Regulation 6(1) states, 'Every employer shall ensure that work equipment is maintained in an efficient state, in working order and in good repair'.

- In today's climate, the matter of supervision and level of reasonable supervision would probably be raised.

Case 50

Activity: Play
Age: Primary
Principle: Inappropriate facility

> **BATES *v* STONE PARISH COUNCIL**
> **Court of Appeal, 1954**
> **3 ALL ER 38, 1 WLR 1249, 52 LGR 469**
> **Lexis**

Summary:

- A four-year-old boy went to a council playground with another young boy. He fell from a slide and sustained severe injuries, which resulted in blindness.

- The slide had a platform about 4 m high. Two horizontal rails were the only safety features for children on the platform. Following a fall approximately 20 years previously, additional rails had been added to safeguard anyone on the platform, but these disappeared over time.

- If council groundsmen saw very young children playing unsupervised on the slide, they sent them away. However, there was no notice prohibiting use of the facility by very young children.

- The claimant fell through the gap between the two rails.

Judgment:

- The council was held liable because of its knowledge of the previous injury and its failure to prevent young children using the facility without appropriate supervision.

- The slide was judged to be dangerous because of the lack of adequate protection on the sides of the platform.

Issues to consider:

- Design of play equipment is governed by much more rigorous standards today.

- Unsupervised use of large-scale play equipment by very young children is far more likely to result in injury than when such children are supervised.

- If equipment or facilities are deemed to hold significant risks when used without supervision, access or use should be prevented until, or unless, supervision can be arranged.

- Repair, and the subsequent adequacy of the equipment, should be confirmed by an appropriate adult before being brought back into use.

Case 51

Activity: Play
Age: Primary
Principle: Securing closed facilities

MORGAN v BLUNDEN and ANOTHER
REILLY v BLUNDEN and ANOTHER
Court of Appeal (Civil Division), 1986
Transcript: Association
Lexis

Summary:

- Two six-year-old children were injured in an adventure playground that was managed by an unincorporated group.

- The playground was part of a larger public open space, separated by a 3 m-high fence with double, padlocked gates. The chain and padlock were regularly vandalised and stolen.

- Supervision was provided during opening hours, with young children left in the care of attendants by their parents. Programmes of supervised activity were advertised. Announcements were sometimes made to say that the playground was closed.

- On the day the injuries occurred, the playground was closed. However, no notification was given to this effect.

- The playground gates were secured by a rope because the lock and chain were missing. However, on the day the children were injured, there was no rope.

- A car had been abandoned in the playground and set on fire. One of the boys inserted a burning stick of wood in the petrol tank of the car, causing an explosion and injuring both boys. There was no evidence of this having happened before.

.

Judgment:

- The claim was dismissed in the first instance because the injuries were not caused by a fault established against the defendants.

- Despite the dismissal, the judge said:

  Those with responsibility for playgrounds open to the use of unaccompanied children have the highest possible duty of care towards such children. They must take every step that a reasonable and humane person would take towards visitors. I find these defendants clearly at fault in leaving the playground in such a state (unlocked)...that children could enter and there disport themselves. Had this plaintiff (claimant) entered when he did and, by playing on a slide or climbing contraption, injured himself, then I can see that these defendants would have a considerable difficulty in defending a claim for damages. In this case, the injury was not caused by any of the appliances.

- It was judged to be an issue of foreseeability. It was argued whether the defendants should have seen the possibility, not the probability, of someone pushing an abandoned car into the playground and setting fire to it. It was judged to be 'unforeseeable to any reasonable occupier that such a dangerous set of circumstances would arise during the two days when the playground was unstaffed'.

- At appeal, it was argued that a breach of duty had been established by not checking that the playground remained secure when it was closed and that liability continued even though the injury occurred 'outside the contemplation of that breach'. This was rejected on the basis that the actual circumstances were beyond reasonable foreseeability: 'A man must be considered to be responsible for the probable consequences of his act. To demand more of him is too harsh a rule.'

- The appeal was also dismissed on the grounds that the accident was of an unforeseeable type.

Issues to consider:

- This judgment reinforces the need to thoroughly and appropriately supervise activities, ensure that equipment is in good order and that, where appropriate, security is effective.

- Staff should be reassured by the reinforcement of the definition of reasonable foreseeability.

Case 52

Activity: Residential trips
Age: Secondary
Principle: Security of accommodation

DICKINSON *v* CORNWALL COUNTY COUNCIL
Exeter County Court, 1999
Zurich Municipal *Court Circular*, March 2000

Summary:

- A 13-year-old girl was raped and murdered in a hostel in France. The parent alleged that the hostel was insecure as the main door was not locked at night.

- The girl shared a dormitory with four other girls.

- The LEA and the school set out detailed organisational guidelines that had been closely followed by the staff involved.

Judgment:

- The claim was dismissed due to the following:
  - The hostel had been used on previous trips without incident.
  - The hostel was situated in a rural, crime-free village where it was customary to leave buildings unlocked.
  - The school and LEA had adhered to detailed checklists when planning the visit.
  - Keys were not issued and bedroom doors were not locked due to the risk of fire.
  - The bedroom windows were open because it was a warm night.
  - Members of staff were sleeping nearby and four other girls were sleeping in the same room as the murdered pupil.

- It was held that the audacity and ferocity of the attack was unforeseeable.

- The judge determined that it was not forseeable that such an event would occur. However, now that it has happened it is forseeable and security of premises needs to be a key aspect of forward planning and ongoing risk assessment.

Issues to consider:

- It is vital to keep the issue of security on school journeys under constant review.

- Accommodation and security arrangements should be checked during pre-visits.

- It is advisable to have the whole pupil group in adjoining rooms, with staff quarters adjacent to these.

- Staff access to pupils' rooms must be available at all times.

- Staff should try to ensure that the accommodation area is for sole use by the group.

- Staff should establish whether 24-hour reception staff are available.

- In order to deter unauthorised visitors, the security arrangements should be checked and the school should be prepared to compensate the system by the use of school staff.

- It is useful to obtain a floor plan of the area designated to the group in advance.

Case 53

Activity: Rugby
Age: Primary
Principle: Unsafe facility

Summary:

- A young boy was playing near rugby posts on a public playing field. A group of older boys were sitting on the crossbar.

- One of the posts fell down, causing the crossbar to hit the boy. This resulted in a head injury and the subsequent risk of epilepsy occurring.

- The posts were made of steel and fitted into a metal sleeve, which was concreted into the ground. It was reported that one of the posts was bent before the accident occurred and that there was rust at the base of the posts.

- The last recorded inspection of the posts was 10 weeks before the accident. Regular checks were made during the playing season but these were fewer during the summer months.

Judgment:

- The judge held that there was a breach of duty by the council as it failed to notice and remedy the rust. The accident was deemed foreseeable.

- The less frequent summer inspections were held to be an 'unjustified lapse', given that there was always a reasonable risk of vandalism.

Issues to consider:

- Eight young people have been killed by unsafe or insecure goalposts in the last 10 years.

- Regular checks should be made to check the stability, condition and security of goalposts – especially portable ones – throughout the period during which the posts are left erected.

- Where potential vandalism may be an issue, checks on facilities such as goalposts should be more frequent and particularly thorough.

Case 54

Activity: Rugby
Age: Adult
Principle: Occupiers' liability and safe *run-off* areas

SIMMS *v* LEIGH FOOTBALL CLUB LTD
Liverpool Autumn Assizes, 1968
(1969) 2 All ER 923
Lexis

Summary:

- A rugby league player broke his leg during a tackle on the touchline. He claimed that the fracture occurred when his leg hit a concrete wall approximately 3.25 m from the touchline.

- The position of the concrete wall complied with the by-laws of the Rugby Football League (RFL) which did not allow boundaries within 3.15 m of the touchline.

- No evidence was found of previous serious injuries of this type and there was no supporting evidence from anyone who may have seen his leg hit the wall.

- The injured player claimed negligence under Section 2 of the Occupiers' Liability Act 1957.

Judgment:

- The claim was dismissed.

- On the balance of probabilities, it was held that the injury was not received during contact with the concrete wall but during the actual tackle, which is an accepted risk when playing rugby.

- It was further stated that, even if the concrete wall had been the cause, the rugby club would not be liable because:

  - Section 2 (1) of the 1957 Act outlines a common duty of care, which was met by the ground. The club had met the specifications set by the RFL, thus, in the words of Justice Wrangham, making the situation, 'though foreseeable, so improbable that it was not necessary to guard against'.

  - Section 2 (5) of the 1957 Act indicates that a duty of care does not impose on an occupier any obligation to a visitor and, in this instance, 'the plaintiff [claimant] must be taken willingly to have accepted the risk of playing on a playing field which, so far as the distance of the wall from the touchline was concerned, complied with the by-laws of the RFL'.

Issues to consider:

- Systems should be established to regularly check areas used for playing games. If the areas are prone to holes, stones, broken glass, animal excreta or other problems (as is common on grass areas today) alternative areas need to be used.

- The Department for Education and Skills (DfES) provides criteria for *run-off* areas on pitches for all sports. These need to be recognised and adhered to for both indoor and outdoor sports, in order to provide a nationally accepted safe area of play. Where such space is not available, risk assessments are needed to determine whether, and in what ways, the activities need to be adapted to maintain a safe environment.

- The placing of mobile goals and other equipment (eg for gymnastics) requires careful thought in order to provide safe working areas that allow for unanticipated movement.

- The provision of padded protection around goalposts and similar equipment during the playing of rugby is good practice.

Case 55

Activity: Skiing
Age: Adult
Principle: Occupiers' liability

OWEN v ROSSENDALE BOROUGH COUNCIL
Telford County Court, 2000
Zurich Municipal *Court Circular*, April 2001

Summary:

- The claimant was injured on an artificial ski slope when he fell, trapping his finger in the honeycombed surface.

- Part of the claim against the council included an allegation of 'failure to display warning signs against the danger of trapped digit injuries in the event of a fall'. It was claimed that the matting design was inherently dangerous.

Judgment:

- The claim was dismissed.

- The judge held the following:
  - Novice skiers are taught how to fall in order to minimise risk.
  - Experienced skiers are aware of the risk.
  - The accident was not caused by inadequate supervision.
  - The matting was not defective.
  - The matting design is in common use with a clear surface.
  - Individuals accept the risks involved in such a high-risk sport.
  - Other slopes do not display warning signs.
  - Injuries of this type cannot be prevented by wearing gloves.

Issues to consider:

- Skiers should be taught how to fall in order to minimise the likelihood of injury.

- Pupils should be taught techniques, in this instance, to minimise the likelihood of falling.

- Appropriate clothing and protection must be worn for adventure activities.

Case 56

Activity: Swimming/diving
Age: Secondary
Principle: Occupiers' liability (before the Act) – adequate warning

---

SIMMONS v THE MAYOR ETC OF THE BOROUGH OF HUNTINGDON
King's Bench Division, 1936
1 All ER 596
Lexis

Summary:

- A 15-year-old boy died when he broke his neck diving from a board into a swimming pool.

- The depth of water was insufficient and no warnings were given, either in notices or by pool-side supervisors.

- The diving board was situated approximately 1 m above the surface of the water. The water was 1 m deep at that point.

Judgment:

- Negligence was proven.

- The placing of the diving board, the insufficient depth of water and the lack of warning amounted to a trap.

- Local authorities, and others providing bathing facilities, are bound to make sure that the safety of bathers is reasonably assured and that there is nothing in the nature of a trap.

- 'There will be considerable divergence of opinion as to what is a safe depth into which a person of average diving ability can dive and providers of pools and such places will be well advised to see there is ample depth, or issue a proper warning of the shallowness of the water.'

Issues to consider:

- Adequate verbal, written and/or visual warning of reasonably foreseeable hazards in the facility should be provided to visitors (including pupils).

- Arrangements should be made for the removal, disablement or *locking out of use* of equipment and facilities that could foreseeably cause serious injury if used at all or without adequate supervision.

- Pupils and other visitors should be taught to recognise and anticipate hazards and to take self-initiated appropriate action, especially in the context of pool-side warnings and advisory notices.

Case 57

Activity: Swimming/diving
Age: Adult
Principle: Owners' liability

PERKOWSKI *v* CITY OF WELLINGTON CORPORATION (N.Z.)
Privy Council, 1958
AC63 (1959); 3 All ER 368 (1958); 3 WLR 564 (1958)
Lexis

Summary:

- The claimant's husband died as a result of injuries suffered when he dived into shallow water from a springboard at low tide in Worser Bay, Wellington, New Zealand.

- No warning signs were evident. The deceased had dived from the springboard on many previous occasions.

- The springboard was in good condition and had been in place for several years. It was not deemed to be a trap.

- The danger was said to arise due to the fact that the sea was shallow outside the area of land occupied by the local council.

- It was accepted by all involved that the deceased was a licensee through the swimming club and not an invitee to the facility. If he had been invited to use the facility, a more general duty of care would have been necessary.

Judgment:

- In the first instance, it was held that the local council was the occupier of the premises that housed the springboard. However, the springboard at low tide was not considered to be a concealed hazard and both parties were considered to have been negligent. The judgment supported the local council, stating that the deceased was 80% responsible for his own death.

- At low tide, the springboard was not deemed to be a concealed hazard as the water was clear and the shallow depth evident.

- The lack of a warning notice was deemed to be negligent.

- The appeal was dismissed.

Issues to consider:

- Pupils cannot be licensees. They are either directed or invited to take part in activities and a general duty of care is owed to them. This requires that they be forewarned of potential hazards, such as the risks of diving from springboards into shallow water.

- The provision of facilities has vastly improved in recent times. It is likely that local councils would remove such facilities, in order to avoid such challenges.

- Pupils' ability to differentiate between real and apparent depths of water should not be relied upon.

Case 58

Activity: Swimming/diving
Age: Adult
Principle: Unsafe facility

DAVIES _v_ THE BOROUGH OF TENBY
Court of Appeal, 1974
2 Lloyd's Rep 469
Lexis

Summary:

- The council erected a high diving board on a rock from which swimmers could dive into the sea.

- The claimant tested the depth of the water before diving and found that he was unable to touch the bottom. Local experts estimated the depth of water at the time to be just 1–1.2 m.

- The diving board was approximately 1.75 m above the water.

- The claimant made two dives without incident. On the third, however, he broke his neck. This resulted in quadriplegia (paralysis of all four limbs) and a life expectancy of 15 years.

- He alleged negligence on the part of the council.

- The council appealed against the judgment, which declared that it was negligent.

Judgment:

- In the first instance, it was inferred by the judge that the depth of the water was 1.8 m. It was also held that the injury was caused either by the claimant diving from the side of the board onto rocks or by slipping on the end of the board due to loose mountings, which caused him to dive deeper than he intended.

- The council was found to be negligent.

- At appeal, there was deemed to be no evidence that the claimant had dived from the side of the board but there was evidence to suggest that the mountings had been loose. The council had thus failed to provide a safe platform from which to dive.

- The claimant was deemed to have contributed to the negligence by not checking that the foothold was secure.

- Appeal judges held that the water was too shallow to dive safely from the high board.

Issues to consider:

- Frequent checking and maintenance of equipment and facilities are essential.
- If the environmental circumstances vary during a particular activity, constant review of the initial risk assessment is necessary to ensure that the facility remains safe to use.
- Faulty equipment should be removed from use immediately. Precautions should be taken to prevent further use until it is adequately repaired or replaced.

Case 59

Activity: Swimming/diving
Age: Adult
Principle: Inadequate attention to the working environment

MCEWAN v EDENIS SAUNASIUM
Court of Appeal (Civil Division), 1986
Transcript: Association
Lexis

Summary:

- An adult claimant suffered serious injury when he dived into a plunge pool at a health club open to the public.

- He hit the back of his head on the bottom of the pool, which rendered him quadriplegic (all four limbs were paralysed). He subsequently died as a result of the injury.

- The pool was small and about 1.2 m deep. 'The size of the pool was such as to suggest that it was of one depth and not a great depth at that.'

- The claimant had consumed between six and eight pints of beer before arriving at the club. However, there was no outward sign that he was affected by the alcohol.

- The claimant had been to the club on one other occasion but had not swum in the pool.

- Outside the club were two posters showing people diving into the water. These were deemed to be misleading in relation to the pool facility provided at the club. One of the posters showed somebody performing a vertical dive.

- The claimant dived in unaware of the depth of the pool. He had not seen any warning notices.

- Bruising on the back of the claimant's head was thought to be due to rotation beyond the vertical during the dive, so that he entered the water turning over. The claimant was judged to have made a running dive, rather than a standing one.

- A claim for negligence under the Occupiers' Liability Act was made against the owners, alleging that diving should not have been allowed.

Judgment:

- In the first instance, the judge held that the pool was 'safe for sensible diving'.

- It was also held that, while the posters were misleading about the facilities at the club, they were not misleading regarding the depth of the pool.

- The level of supervision (which was undefined) was deemed to be adequate.

- The main issue centred on the alleged failure to provide proper warning about the depth of the pool, through inadequate notices and the cloudy condition of the water.

- The notices were deemed to be adequate, unlike the clarity of the water. However, the lack of clarity did not cause the dangerous dive and subsequent accident. The claimant paid no particular attention to the condition of the pool before he performed a running dive. The clarity of the water would have made no difference to the outcome as the diver was committed to the action before being able to assess the water.

- The appeal was dismissed. The owners of the pool were not negligent. Instead, the claimant 'did not apply his mind to the question of the depth of the pool as he dived'.

Issues to consider:

- Young people should be taught to assess the circumstances of their environment and activity before committing themselves to an action. They need to be attentive to the task in hand.

- Running dives should not be allowed in class situations and should be strongly discouraged in leisure situations. Running dives do not allow adequate time for performers to assess the situation and amend their intended action before being committed to it.

- Adequate notices about the water depth in pools should be clearly displayed. Adequate warning, visually and verbally, should also be provided.

- Pools in which the condition of the water prevents a clear view of the bottom of the pool should not be used.

Case 60

Activity: Swimming
Age: Adult
Principle: Design of facilities

BAINS v YORK CITY COUNCIL
Court of Appeal, 1992
Transcript: Association
Lexis

Summary:

- An adult woman entered the shallow end of a pool by the steps in the conventional way, facing the pool edge.

- The steps were of a conventional design. The tubular handrails had treads of 10 cm wide and there was a 10 cm gap between the steps and the pool wall.

- The woman's foot slipped off the edge of a step and into the gap. This resulted in a severe sprain.

- She challenged under both a duty of care in negligence and Section 2 (2) of the Occupiers' Liability Act 1957, which states that the occupier should 'take such care as is reasonable to see that the visitor will be reasonably safe in using the premises for the purposes for which he is invited or permitted by the occupier to be there...and the degree of care, and want of care, which would ordinarily be looked for in such a visitor'.

- There had been four million visitors to the pool since its opening and, in that time, no similar incidents were recorded. In fact, there was no evidence of similar accidents occurring anywhere.

Judgment:

- The local council was held liable in the first instance but this was overturned at appeal.

- The original judgment identified the gap between the step and the wall as a foreseeable risk that needed to be eliminated.

- The *appeal court* reversed the decision because the design was deemed to be appropriate and there was no evidence of previous similar incidents, thus determining that the accident was not foreseeable and there was no liability.

Issues to consider:

- *Regular and approved practice* (or, in this case, design) should be implemented. Careful thought should be given before adapting or improvising equipment as this weakens one's position in the event of an injury and the case going to court.

- It is important that pupils are taught the correct methods of using equipment or facilities, through close monitoring to ensure that the correct mode of use is maintained.

- A visual check of equipment and facilities being used is advisable, whether on the school site or at another location, to monitor any possible deterioration or defect before pupils begin work.

Case 61

Activity: Swimming/diving
Age: Adult
Principle: Occupiers' liability

O'SHEA v ROYAL BOROUGH OF KINGSTON-UPON-THAMES
Court of Appeal, 1994
John Larking
Lexis

Summary:

- A man dived from a freeboard (0.5 m in height) into water of 1.3 m in depth. The distance from the pool side to the water level is usually approximately 0.2 m. He entered head first with his arms by his sides and struck his head on the pool bottom. He is now a quadriplegic (all four of his limbs are paralysed).

- The pool was a hybrid leisure pool, with a beach area and very shallow water and a wave machine. There was also a conventional end with marked race lanes. It was the injured man's first visit to this particular pool.

- The water depth was marked in small print on the pool walls, at just above water level. The man had not noticed the depth signs. There were four pool-side supervisors on duty.

- Local Authority Pool Regulations stated that, 'due to the shallow nature of the pool, diving is not advisable'. Rules for pool-side staff also prohibited diving into the shallow area of the pool and required staff to 'always advise clients to use a shallow style dive'.

Judgment:

- The local authority was found to be liable for negligence and breach of statutory duty under Section 2 of the Occupiers' Liability Act 1957.

- It was held that the local authority was negligent as it did not prohibit diving and failed to instruct the pool-side staff to enforce such prohibition. It was held that the only safe course of action was to prohibit diving.

- It was also held that the man contributed equally to the injury by:
  - failing to heed the depth of the water
  - diving in with his hands by his sides
  - failing to perform a shallow dive.

- Liability and contributory negligence were confirmed at appeal.

- Judge Neill said:

No doubt numerically the chances of a serious accident are small...yet there is a risk of catastrophic injury if one considers the type of pool and the fact that people will come to the pool who are not expert divers. We must consider the difficulty of supervised restricted diving. The ban with which we are concerned is one that would have been applied in uncontrolled (public) sessions and which might have been removed or modified if organised racing had been taking place or a swimmer was being taught by a qualified instructor.

Issues to consider:

- When using a public pool, the following guidelines should be adhered to:

  - Safety equipment and signs should be checked to ensure that they are present and prominent.

  - The pool's safety regulations should be checked and, if necessary, staff should impose more specific and stringent requirements on the school group.

  - The group should be regularly reminded of the safety requirements.

  - Diving should not be allowed if the freeboard is greater than the common 20–30 cm.

  - The national guidelines that were established in 1990, following this incident, should be stringently followed. The current Amateur Swimming Association guidelines should be checked for the necessary depths of water that are required for racing, shallow and vertical dives.

Case 62

Activity: Swimming/diving
Age: Adult
Principle: Occupiers' liability – unauthorised access

> **RATCLIFF v MCCONNELL and OTHERS**
> **Court of Appeal, 1998**
> **1 WLR 670 1999**
> **Lexis**

Summary:

- A 19-year-old student and two friends went swimming in the college's open-air pool at night, despite knowing it was not allowed and that the pool was closed for the winter.

- The student had been drinking but was not drunk.

- Half the pool length was shallow, before sloping downwards to a depth of 4 m. It was surrounded by substantial walls of 2 m in height, fences and a locked gate. Notices stated clearly that the pool was closed. The only lighting was a motion-activated security light. Notices indicating depth were clear and notices at the deep end said, 'Deep end shallow dive'.

- The claimant climbed over the gate, dived in and hit his head on the bottom, suffering severe injuries. He subsequently suffered quadriplegia (paralysis of all four limbs).

- The student admitted to the following:
  - He knew that the pool was closed.
  - He knew that access to the pool was prohibited.
  - He had a wide knowledge of pools.
  - He was aware that diving could be dangerous.
  - He knew that it was dangerous to dive into water of an unknown depth.

- The student did not know where the variations in pool depth occurred or whether it might be safe to dive. He knew that the water level was low.

- The student sued the college for breach of duty under the Occupiers' Liability Act 1984.

- The college denied that the student was a lawful visitor to the pool, denied negligence and pleaded *volenti non fit injuria* and contributory negligence.

- It emerged that the college representatives were aware that the pool had been used regularly by students during prohibited hours and that no disciplinary measures had been taken in previous years. This was rectified four years before the incident and abuse of the rules had stopped. No measures were taken to forewarn new students and visitors of the hours of use of the pool, that the pool was unsafe for diving or that diving should have been prohibited.

Judgment:

- The college was initially held liable subject to 40% contributory negligence by the student, because the college did not give warnings of the danger or discourage people from taking the risk. The college appealed.

- The appeal was granted and the original decision reversed.

- The Court of Appeal determined that a duty was owed to an individual trespasser only if the occupier was aware of the danger or had reasonable grounds to believe that it existed, that the risk (of injury from diving into shallow water) was common in all pools and was obvious to any adult. The college, as an occupier, was under no duty to protect the student against apparent dangers of which he should have been fully aware. The claimant was fully aware of the risk and willingly accepted it – the college thus had no duty to the student in this situation.

Issues to consider:

- A duty is owed to trespassers if a risk or danger is known or is reasonably foreseeable.

- Consideration should be given to risk assessments of what may occur in a situation of trespass, in order to ensure that reasonably foreseeable trespass could be prevented.

- The importance of notices indicating that a facility is closed or entry is prohibited, and notices relating to the facility (eg depth, no diving) cannot be over-emphasised. Also, if relevant, notices indicating that a potential hazard exists (eg low water level) are vital.

- Facilities that are *out of use* need to be securely locked and/or access prevented in other ways as far as is reasonably possible.

- Ongoing risk assessments are necessary if the conditions of pool usage change in school pools, especially during the holidays when trespass may occur.

Case 63

Activity: Swimming/diving
Age: Adult
Principle: Occupiers' liability – reasonable precautions

**TOMLINSON v CONGLETON DISTRICT COUNCIL and
CHESHIRE COUNTY COUNCIL**
Queen's Bench, Manchester, 2000
Zurich Municipal *Court Circular*, **July 2001 and** *Daily Mail*, **4 August 2003**

Summary:

- Cheshire County Council managed an old sandpit lake on behalf of its owners, Congleton District Council. At its deepest, the lake was approximately 35 m. The bottom shelved at varying degrees from the shoreline. Its sandy beaches made it a popular summertime venue for the public.

- The district council had long recognised the definite risk of drowning in the lake. Signs indicating the dangers and prohibiting swimming were increased but ignored.

- The claimant dived in, hit his head on the bottom and broke his neck. He said he was unaware that swimming was not allowed.

- The claimant could not see through the water to the bottom. He accepted that he should not have dived. He assumed that the lake was of a sufficient depth without checking. He claimed that the council should have taken more steps to protect the public.

Judgment:

- The case was dismissed in the first instance but the district council was held responsible at appeal with a discount of two thirds for contributory negligence. 'A duty of care was owed to offer *some* protection.' Warning notices prohibiting swimming were evident and council staff remonstrated with offenders. It was the court's view that further steps should have been taken.

- On further appeal to the House of Lords in 2003, the case was dismissed. While accepting that the claimant had suffered a terrible tragedy, the Law Lords unanimously ruled against him on the grounds that the council had displayed warning signs and rangers patrolled the area. 'There is some risk of accidents arising out of the *joie de vivre* of the young but it is no reason for imposing a grey and dull safety regime on everyone.'

- It was held that the risk posed when diving was obvious and that there was no common law duty or statutory duty to warn of such a risk. The risk to users came from engaging in dangerous activity and not from anything done or not done by the council.

- People were free to make a choice whether or not to ignore the signs that were warning of the danger. They could choose to accept the risk. The claimant was deemed to be a person of full capacity who voluntarily engaged in the dangerous activity of diving into an unknown depth of water.

- The Occupiers' Liability Act 1957 requires the occupier to safeguard the visitor 'for the purpose of which he is invited or permitted to be there'. When the claimant entered the water and dived, he ceased to be there for the purposes he was allowed by the occupier. Occupiers have no legal duty 'to protect persons of full capacity from injury if they are voluntarily and irresponsibly subjecting themselves to obvious danger'.

- Making the lake safer by fencing it off 'would have prevented the majority of people from enjoying normal activities that were permitted on the land in order to protect those that were putting themselves at obvious risk'.

Issues to consider:

- The Court of Appeal judgment had implications as extreme as fencing off all lakes and ponds in Britain – a totally impractical action. The House of Lords' dismissal recognises that safety advice is necessary but that it is impossible to cater for every situation that puts an unrealistic burden on the proprietors of leisure and school facilities.

- There is no legal obligation for owners/occupiers to take extreme measures to prevent use, beyond what would be deemed as reasonable forewarning.

- Responsible adults must act on behalf of young people when considering allowing them access to open water or other facilities.

5.4 CASES OF NEGLIGENCE RELATING TO CONTEXT: EQUIPMENT

Case 64

Activity: Cricket
Age: Secondary
Principle: Personal protection

LOTT *v* DEVON COUNTY COUNCIL
Torquay County Court, 2000
Zurich Municipal *Court Circular*, July 2001

Summary:

- The claimant was a late order batsman in a competitive cricket match.

- The opposition included a very good fast bowler.

- When the claimant began his innings, he faced a bowler of moderate pace.

- Protective helmets were available but had not been recommended by the school staff for facing the moderate bowler. It is important to note that this incident occurred prior to the England and Wales Cricket Board's (ECB) directive on helmets.

- The bareheaded claimant suffered injury when struck by a ball that was bowled by the moderate opponent.

Judgment:

- The claim was dismissed.

- The judge held that the school had followed all the recommendations then in place from the ECB.

- The bowler involved in the incident was deemed to be a trundler, not someone dangerous against whom special precautions should be taken. 'One or two errant deliveries would not have been sufficient to make the wearing of helmets obligatory in this game.'

Issues to consider:

- Risk assessment is necessary in order to judge the levels of skill involved in relation to the quality of the facility available.

- School staff should keep abreast of current guidelines and follow these where mandatory, or take account of appropriate guidance when carrying out risk assessments.

- The inclusion of a very good, fast bowler in a cricket team indicates the need to have appropriate personal protection to hand to use when necessary. If there is any doubt, cricket helmets should be worn.

Case 65

Activity: Gymnastics
Age: Primary
Principle: Inappropriate apparatus for age of pupils

BUTLER v CHESHIRE COUNTY COUNCIL
County Court, 1996

Summary:

- A six-year-old pupil fell approximately 1.5 m from a climbing frame during a physical education lesson.

- The size of the class was considered to be reasonable and the teacher was described as careful, caring and someone who knew the class well. The children were not unruly.

- There had only been one accident on climbing frames during the previous two years in the whole of the county's 450 schools. This was typical of national figures.

- A claim for negligent supervision by the teacher was alleged. It was also argued that the climbing frame apparatus was inappropriate for the age of the child.

Judgment:

- The claim was dismissed.

- The climbing frame was deemed to be adequate, being of typical construction with no indication that it was slippery. Justice Lachs said:

  When one looks at the risks of the climbing frame in question, it is clear that the risk is very small. It is a safe piece of equipment and it is a credit to teachers that they exercise such supervision as to prevent more accidents...Equipment of this height (3 m) does not present any danger at all to children in these schools.

- There was no evidence that the equipment was faulty or that the teacher was negligent. According to Lachs:

  The idea that each child should be supervised at each moment is wrong. She [the teacher] positioned herself in the gym in the position where she was able to view all her class. If, without warning, a child falls, then what can a teacher do? A teacher cannot take anticipatory action, and catch a child, in the fleeting second that it takes a child to fall.

Issues to consider:

- The equipment provided in schools by an LEA is appropriate for the needs of that type of school. The staff need to facilitate progressive, guided experience of the full range of available equipment.

- Good positioning to enable the responsible adult to view the whole class, observation and analysis of what is happening plus appropriate intervention, if deemed to be necessary, are crucial.

- Proven maintenance and equipment inspection is required on an annual basis.

Case 66

Activity: Gymnastics
Age: Primary
Principle: Appropriate equipment

PEEL v ASHFIELD GYMNASTICS CLUB
Mansfield County Court, 2001

Summary:

- A nine-year-old girl was injured during a voluntary artistic gymnastics club training session. She had attended the club two or three times a week for approximately three years.

- Four regular and qualified coaches took the training session, one of whom had overall responsibility.

- The injury occurred on a set of asymmetric bars. Mats were positioned beneath and beyond the bars. In addition, a weight-absorbent safety mattress was used to accommodate dismount landings from the higher bar, which was approximately 2.5 m in height. The size of the safety mattress at the time was disputed. It had been replaced before litigation commenced.

- The claimant had successfully practised the bar sequence and dismount in previous training sessions. On the occasion of the injury, the claimant adjusted the position of the mattress to accommodate an intended increase in flight from her dismount. It was common practice to adjust the safety mattress to accommodate individual performances.

- At the conclusion of the sequence, the claimant released her grip from the high bar slightly too late, resulting in the flight-off being too vertical. She landed with part of her foot on the mattress and part off it, resulting in a serious ankle fracture.

- It was claimed that the safety mattress was not large enough to accommodate the dismount landing. No other similar injuries had occurred in 25 years of coaching.

Judgment:

- The claim was dismissed.

- The level and conduct of the coaching was judged to be acceptable.

Issues to consider:

- Serious injury may occur when, in performing a high-momentum landing, a pupil lands on the edge of a thick weight-absorbent safety mattress. The greatest care should be taken to avoid this.

- Weight-absorbent safety mattress landing areas should be of a sufficient size in order to avoid the need for gymnasts to adjust their positions.

- It is helpful to record all accidents and, when deemed good practice, to adjust organisation and management techniques.

Case 67

Activity: Gymnastics
Age: Secondary
Principle: Inadequate disposal of condemned equipment

BEAUMONT v SURREY COUNTY COUNCIL
Queen's Bench, 1968
66 LGR 580
Lexis

Summary:

- A physical education teacher left an old trampette elastic in a school playground wastepaper bin.

- During the morning break, a group of boys found the elastic and, during horseplay, another boy was hit in the eye by the elastic, losing his sight in that eye.

- The school playground duty system involved two teachers and prefects clearing the classrooms and supervising the playground. On that particular day, the duty staff were delayed in clearing the classrooms and were not out in the playground when the incident occurred.

- The LEA was sued for negligence on the basis that:
  - it was foreseeable that, by leaving the elastic in the bin, incorporating it into horseplay could result in injury
  - insufficient supervision was provided in the playground at the time of the incident.

Judgment:

- The LEA was held to be negligent, according to Justice Lane, on the following counts:
  - 'It was the headmaster's duty, bearing in mind the known propensities of boys and girls between the ages of 11 and 18, to take all reasonable and proper steps to prevent any of the pupils under his care from suffering injury from inanimate objects, from actions of their fellow pupils, or from a combination of both.'
  - 'It was unreasonable to put the powerful elastic in the open waste paper bin...and the horseplay would have been stopped before the accident occurred if the system of supervision had been working properly.'

- The system was thus deemed to be adequate but not effectively carried out on that day.

Issues to consider:

- Faulty equipment should be removed from use immediately. Precautions should be taken to prevent further use until it is adequately repaired or replaced.

- Systems and procedures, as per school documentation, should be followed. If a system, procedure or duty cannot be implemented, senior management should be informed immediately. Compensatory action can then be initiated.

- Risk assessments need to be carried out and regularly reviewed in order to accommodate any aspects where risk is deemed to remain.

- This case is reported to have raised the standard of care expected. The judgment made three references to this being a high standard.

Case 68

Activity: Gymnastics
Age: Secondary
Principle: Using equipment for the purpose it was designed

TAPPING v KENT COUNTY COUNCIL
Queen's Bench Division, 1990
WH Clark
Lexis

Summary:

- An 11-year-old boy seriously fractured and dislocated the elbow of his dominant arm while performing a gate vault over a height of 1.2 m. This caused a degree of permanent disability.

- The class was described as being properly instructed and competent in the use of the equipment.

- A claim for negligence was made on the basis of injury occurring during a race 'with an element of competition and haste'. The boy fell onto his elbow directly on the floor because displaced mats had not been replaced in the correct positions. The physical education specialist disputed each claim.

Judgment:

- Liability for injury was held – the teacher was negligent.

- The following was determined:

   - A race was in progress. Justice Tucker said, 'The teacher organised a race between the groups with the pieces of apparatus operating as obstacles around the course. The last team to complete the course would have to perform press-ups as a forfeit for losing.'

   - The boy fell onto his elbow, which was confirmed by orthopaedic evidence.

   - The mats had moved, exposing an area of bare floor onto which the boy fell, caused by 'the speed and competitiveness at which the boys were using the apparatus'.

- The judge was influenced in his decision by the teacher's 'disquieting vagueness and evasiveness in his answers...and on the written accident reports' as opposed to the pupils, who gave evidence in a straight forward, direct and honest manner.

Issues to consider:

- Chasing games, obstacle races and other competitive activities over gymnastic apparatus are not using the equipment for the purpose it was designed.

- It is foreseeable that competitive races or chasing games over apparatus, such as Pirates, place pressure on the pupils who, in haste, may fall from the apparatus.

- When mats are used to provide cushioned landing areas, stringent observation and action by staff, and pupils who have been taught to handle such situations, are necessary to ensure that the mats are immediately repositioned should they move. This may require a temporary halt to the activity.

- Accident report forms should be completed with clarity and detail. Diagrams and additional notes may prove to be advantageous and are considered good practice.

- Imposing forfeits for the last individual or group to finish a task (eg press-ups) has no educational value and creates an inappropriate, pressurised situation.

Case 69

Activity: Gymnastics
Age: Adult
Principle: Accessibility of equipment outside normal sessions without qualified supervision

FOWLES v BEDFORDSHIRE COUNTY COUNCIL
Court of Appeal, 1995
The Times, **22 June 1995, J Larking**
Lexis

Summary:

- A 21-year-old man regularly attended a youth centre, set up as the 'antithesis of a school', for young people with social problems and low self-esteem. The centre included an activities room for table tennis, badminton, weights and trampolining, which housed gymnastics mats.

- One of the supervisors, who was qualified to teach trampolining but not gymnastics, had taught the man a forward somersault on the trampoline and had developed this, with support, on the mats in the centre of the hall.

- During a visit to the centre, the man and a friend went to the activities room and, without supervision, set up the safety mattress abutted against a wall. They proceeded to perform forward somersaults.

- The man put extra effort into one attempt for the benefit of a small audience. He over-rotated, catapulted into the wall and was seriously injured. He is now quadriplegic (all four limbs are paralysed).

- The position of the mat was such that the centre of it was only approximately 1 m from the wall.

- The injured man charged the County Council with negligence for personal injury and for a breach of statutory care under Section 2 of the Occupiers' Liability Act 1957. This was on the basis that the mats had not been made inaccessible without supervision.

Judgment:

- It was held that the County Council was not liable under Section 2 of the 1957 Act. Judge Millet said:

  As occupiers of the premises, the defendants owed Mr Fowles a duty not to expose him to dangers due to the state of the premises or to things done or omitted to be done on the premises, whether by themselves or by other visitors. But the accident did not occur as a result of a breach of any such duty. They were under no duty as occupiers to take steps to prevent their visitors harming themselves by their own foolish conduct whilst on the premises. The availability of the mat did not cause the accident in any relevant sense; it merely provided Mr Fowles with the opportunity to cause himself harm.

- It was held that the County Council was liable for negligence:
  - The coach was not qualified to teach gymnastics. Expert opinion stated that a coach of Level 4 ability needed to be present at all times when a forward somersault was being taught or performed.
  - Those wishing to learn the forward somersault should have the theory and inherent dangers carefully explained to them (there is no national or legal requirement to be qualified to teach specific activities. Employers' requirements for the necessary qualifications to teach any activity to any level should be checked).
  - Instruction had not been given regarding the proper use of weight-absorbent safety matresses. The sole cause of the accident was identified as the placement of the mat hard up against the wall.
  - No participants had been expressly prohibited from attempting hazardous gymnastic activities without supervision – no written warning, notice or verbal instruction was given.
- It was also held that the man had contributed to the injury through his negligence, to a level of two-thirds of the blame. He was almost six feet tall and 'the danger of his hitting the wall if he placed the mat where he did must have been obvious to him'.

Issues to consider:

- Effective supervision is essential when pupils are involved in any activity that is deemed to be potentially hazardous.

- The judgment made a distinction between youth centres and schools in relation to securing equipment, stating that 'the duty of care of the occupiers at the youth centre, as opposed to a school, did not extend to the removal and securing of the mats, except when in use under immediate supervision'. In schools, equipment should thus be made secure outside lessons. This is most effectively achieved by locking facilities, storerooms and changing rooms.

- As pupils are both young and diverse in their skills, it is likely that schools allowing gymnastic equipment to be readily available without supervision will be negligent, regardless of the cautionary or prohibitive notices that have been displayed and the previous instructions that have been given.

- Schools need to regularly review their procedures.

- The plant, systems of work and procedures for health on site must be safe for both visitors and those working there. This is the responsibility of those *controlling* non-domestic premises (ie governors, head teachers and school staff).

Case 70

Activity: Hockey
Age: Secondary
Principle: Safe use of equipment

CASSIDY v THE COUNCIL OF THE CITY OF MANCHESTER
Court of Appeal, 1995
John Larking
Lexis

Summary:

- A 13-year-old girl fractured her elbow falling over the leg of a bench that was laid on its side. The bench had been turned on its side approximately 1–2 m from the back wall as a goal for a four-a-side indoor hockey match during a physical education lesson.

- Leaning against the back wall was a five-a-side football goal and net.

- The ball went behind the upturned bench during the game. The girl rushed to collect it and tripped over the legs of the bench.

- The teacher's instructions were general regarding how to play the game and taking care while playing.

Judgment:

- The LEA was found negligent on the basis of inadequate supervision and breaching its duty under the Occupiers' Liability Act, by a failure to provide proper and safe equipment.

- The court rejected the defence that 'the use of the bench in this way was the normal and common practice in physical education classes throughout the country and was not unsafe'. Instead, the court held that there was no evidence produced that it was common practice to use the bench in this way: 'A bench in that position, with 13-year-olds dashing about the gym was a potential hazard. In her hurry to retrieve the ball she had allowed herself to overlook the hazard and tripped over and injured herself'.

- It is significant that the *appeal court* held that the court in the first instance was entitled to reach the judgment it did on the evidence placed before it. This was a particular reference to the lack of sufficient proof by the defence that improvising a goal or target by turning a bench on its side was widely used, in order to constitute *regular and approved practice*. This distinguishes the situation from the case of *Wright v Cheshire County Council 1952*, where *regular and approved practice* was established.

Issues to consider:

- The organisation and presentation of lessons should be based on *regular and approved practice* – that which has been used widely and over a sufficient period of time, and is therefore shown to be safe if organised properly.

- Pupils should be warned of specific hazards. Such warnings should not be simply left at a general level. This requires risk assessments to be carried out and regularly reviewed.

- Using benches turned on their sides as targets or goals is very common. Usually, they are pushed against the wall so that pupils are unable to get behind them. The distance between the bench and the wall is the distinguishing factor in this case. The pupil was able to get behind the bench and stumble over it.

Case 71

Activity: Outdoor adventure activities
Age: Secondary
Principle: Inappropriate activity with inappropriate equipment

RAMSAY v KINGS SCHOOL and MINISTRY OF DEFENCE (MoD)
Lincoln County Court, 1999

Summary:

- A 12-year-old boy attended a Year 7 three-day camp and adventure activity programme at an army range under the control of the Army Youth Team.

- Through the Army Youth Team, the Ministry of Defence (MoD) provided the accommodation, facilities, equipment and instruction.

- During a mountain biking activity, the claimant descended a hill and lost control of the bike. He fell off and fractured his arm.

- The claimant sued the school for failing to properly assess the mountain biking activity in relation to its suitability for inexperienced 11–12 year-olds. He also claimed that the staff had not considered the risks involved when the pupils experienced difficulties with the course during the activity and had not reassessed or modified the activity. He also alleged inadequate supervision by school staff and other adults.

- The claimant sued the MoD for similar causes as well as for providing poorly maintained equipment, for failing to familiarise the group with the course and for not advising the group to dismount and walk when the demands of the course were beyond them.

- When the group of nine pupils was involved in the activity, only one adult (an army instructor) was with the group. A member of staff who should have been with them remained at the base because a pupil was ill.

- The group was told to choose a bike. The pupils were not matched by height or previous experience. The claimant chose a bike that had faulty gears and brakes but he did not report this.

- At the top of a steep slope, the group was told to take care due to previous incidents and to descend the hill at 10-second intervals. Another boy fell during this descent.

- The claimant pushed his bike down a particularly steep section but was told to hurry up. When riding this section he lost control, hit a rock, fell off and was injured.

- The group as a whole reported the attitudes of the army instructors as 'unhelpful', the bikes as poorly maintained and generally too big for those in the group, and the course as very steep and demanding.

- The teacher in charge had cycled the course and felt it was safe.

- Staff had visited the centre prior to the course.

- The army provided evidence of the bikes being serviced and maintained. Staff were qualified and set procedures were followed.

Judgment:

- The course was unsuitable for the age and experience of the pupils involved.

- The group had not been given any preview of the slope and thus were in no position to decide whether to walk or cycle.

- The army instructor was deemed to have little experience of working with young people – his training related to working with adults. He had little experience of teaching mountain biking.

- The school and the MoD were held to be jointly negligent.

Issues to consider:

- Adult helpers working with groups should be experienced in the demands of the age group, activity and environment before assuming sole charge.

- A preview by pupils before any section of a particular challenge in an activity is important so that they do not participate *blindly*.

- Activities should be carefully matched to levels of experience.

- Risk assessments should be carried out at the planning stage and should be constantly reviewed during an activity.

- Nobody should be afraid to say 'stop'.

- Military qualifications are specific to the needs of the military and may not be appropriate in terms of understanding young peoples' development and capabilities. When pupils attend military-organised events, school staff continue to be responsible for them. Staff must be satisfied with the standards and attitudes of the instructional staff. This also applies to the use of commercial companies, such as ski schools.

Case 72

Activity: Play
Age: Pre-school
Principle: Inadequate security of equipment

COATES v RAWTENSTALL BOROUGH COUNCIL
Manchester Assizes, 1957
1 ALL ER 333
Lexis

Summary:

- A three-year-old claimant and a boy aged 14 were injured on a slide in a local authority recreation ground. A chain had been improperly fixed across the slide by another child. The three-year-old broke his thigh and paralysis developed later.

- The chain was officially used to prevent use of the slide on Sundays (this took place in 1956). On this occasion, it had not been properly secured by the playground attendant, thus another child was able to remove it and use it inappropriately.

- The local council contended that the playground was for use only by children of school age and that this made the very young child a trespasser. It was argued for the claimant that he was an invitee with rights.

Judgment:

- It was held that the child was not trespassing and was owed a duty of care as no steps were taken to prevent very young children using the playground (eg there were no local by-laws regulating the use of the playground).

- The judge quoted an earlier case: 'The authority is liable if it provides "traps". It would be liable for defective or dangerous premises or implements for play'.

- The judge stated:

  The public have a right to go to the playground. It is the duty of the local authority to do something more than...that arising from the cold neutrality of a land owner who allows persons to visit his property. The occupier is bound not to create a trap or allow a concealed danger to exist upon the said premises which is not apparent to the visitor but which is known – or ought to be known – to the occupier.

- It was held that the slide with the chain across it constituted a trap because the council's employee did not adequately secure the chain to prevent misuse. The employee 'ought reasonably to have anticipated intervention by mischievous boys.' The council was thus held to be liable for the injury.

Issue to consider:

• Systems should be implemented in order to ensure that children are unable to place themselves in *exceptional danger* through avoidable access to potentially hazardous situations. For example, these situations may be avoided by locking or disabling trampolines and trampettes to prevent unauthorised use.

Case 73

Activity: Play
Age: Pre-school
Principle: Inappropriate equipment

Summary:

- A three-year-old sustained a serious injury in a council play park in 1980. It took over 20 years for the case to reach court.

- The claimant faces lifelong effects and possibly surgery throughout his life from the results of the injury.

- The allegations of injury were undermined by the hospital admission notes, which recorded a fall from a rocking horse. This conflicted with the claim that the child had been standing at the rear of the horse; that he was holding its frame; that he was jerked up in the air by its violent movement; and that the horse landed heavily on his knee as it swung down again.

- Inadequate ground clearance of the horse in action was claimed.

- A publication produced by reputable bodies and entitled *Danger in the Playground*, recommended that play horses should be fixed and not able to rock.

- The claimant was not accompanied by an adult at the time of the accident. He had been entrusted to a 12-year-old friend.

Judgment:

- The claim was dismissed.

- The judge did not accept the claimant's version of events, due to the medical records available.

- The judge referred to the British Standards guidance, which stated that rocking horses were recognised items in play parks, while also stating that British Standards 'represent good practice but they are not prescriptive'.

Issues to consider:

- The time it took for the case to come to court may seem astounding. However, it falls within the time allowed for individuals to make retrospective claims, which is within three years of coming of age as an adult.

- This case highlights the importance of keeping records and evidence until a statutory time bar takes effect.

- Minors cannot assume responsibility for the actions of very young children who may be placed in their care. This is an issue relating to the responsibilities that may, wrongly, be placed on young people with leadership experience.

5.5 CASES OF NEGLIGENCE RELATING TO ACTIVITY ORGANISATION: PREPARATION

Case 74

Activity: Assault courses
Age: Secondary
Principle: Adequate preparation and precautions to satisfy duty of care

> **MORGAN v AVONHURST SCHOOL EDUCATION TRUST**
> **Court of Appeal (Civil Division), 1995**
> **Transcript: Association**
> **Lexis**

Summary:

- A Combined Cadet Force (CCF) gave a demonstration on an assault course, typical of that used by the army for recruits but set up in the middle of Bristol. Some modifications were made to accommodate this while still simulating army conditions.

- A simulated rock face 4 m high was constructed against a convenient bank. The intention was that the cadets would run along the top of the bank and over the simulated rock face. A rope was provided to aid descent from the rock face by abseiling. Thin gymnastic mats were spread on the floor.

- Four teams were competing in the race.

- The 17-year-old claimant took part in his own team and either volunteered or was directed to also take the place of a missing cadet in another team, thus participating in the shortened course 14 times during the race. He had a rest of between 15 and 20 minutes between each circuit.

- On the last circuit, the claimant slipped while descending the rock face on the rope, breaking both wrists.

- The claimant sued his school and the Ministry of Defence (MoD), alleging that the course had not been set up properly. The school had had nothing to do with setting up the course.

Judgment:

- The claim was dismissed in the first instance and also by the Court of Appeal.

- Reasonable precautions, with mats and rope, had been taken for trained and fit cadets.

- It was held that, 'if thicker, foam mattresses at the base of the rock face had been provided, the whole point of the assessment course would have been thwarted...and the positioning of someone at the foot of the wall to catch anyone who happened to slip or fall...would have created more danger than it would have prevented'.

- The judge decided that the claimant was fit and suffered no undue physical strain in completing 14 short circuits with a period of rest in between.

- This was deemed to be a military exercise, rather than a gymnastic display.

Issues to consider:

- Staff should ensure that pupils are sufficiently prepared, physically and technically, for the demands of any task set.

- It should be carefully considered whether races over equipment are advisable at any time. In a gymnastic rather than military context, this judgment may well have been very different.

- It is important to consider whether the placement of support will help or adversely affect the safety of the task.

- Schools maintain the responsibility to ensure that pupils are not exposed to unacceptable levels of risk, whether or not school staff are directly responsible for leading the activity.

Case 75

Activity: Climbing
Age: Adult
Principle: Progressive experience

POPE v CUTHBERTSON
Queen's Bench Division, 1995
Transcript
Lexis

Summary:

- An adult fell and was injured while rock climbing. He alleged negligent discharge of duties against his instructor.

- The instructor was a member of the Association of Mountain Guides and was subsequently very experienced and well qualified.

- The adult had the equivalent of approximately 30 days of climbing experience. Almost all of the experience had been gained under the guidance and instruction of fully qualified guides. On some, he led the climbs.

- The claimant asked to lead a climb. The guide assessed his ability over two days and then allowed the adult to lead on the third. He fell on the second pitch of the second climb he was leading.

Judgment:

- The claim was dismissed – there was no evidence of failure to instruct or supervise that could have contributed to the accident.

- The court was satisfied with the guide's ability and experience. It was held that the guide took a cautionary approach to allowing the adult to lead.

- The court referred to inconsistencies in the claimant's witness statements before and during the trial. Judgment was influenced by this unreliability. Deputy Justice Cotton said, 'At the outset, his determination to recover compensation from the defendant caused him to represent events in the way he thought most likely to advance his case, rather than as they actually were'.

- It was accepted that, during the climb, the guide had threaded an element of instruction, which included the placement of suitable and secure protection. The failure of the *friend*, which caused the adult to fall, was not held to be the responsibility of the guide who had required the adult leader to make it more secure before relying on it.

- It was also accepted that the guide controlled the rope during the adult's fall as best he could and did not fall short of the high standards of care expected of a skilled mountain guide.

Issues to consider:

- Staff members must acknowledge and understand the dangers, and accept the risk involved in adventure activities. They should not seek to offload responsibility onto others.

- Members of staff who are responsible for young (and possibly inexperienced) pupils should check all equipment, facilities and conditions before and during the activities.

- School staff and coaches should be well experienced and, where possible, well qualified in activities which may be potentially hazardous to young people.

- Pupils need to progress through rigorous training and assessment processes before enjoying any degree of independence or responsibility, such as leading a climb.

Case 76

Activity: Climbing
Age: Adult
Principle: Regular and approved practice

WOODROFFE-HEDLEY *v* CUTHBERTSON
High Court, 1997
Sports Law, Administration and Practice – **Informa Professional Publications**
September 1997, 4:6

Summary:

- An experienced alpine climber was alleged to have caused the death of a client by not following regular and approved practice.

- The son of the deceased brought the action against the defendant under the Fatal Accidents Act 1976. This Act is based on the usual principles of negligence.

- The facts of the case were not disputed.

- The client was an experienced climber but inexperienced in ice climbing.

- The incident occurred after a few successful ascents.

- The role of leader and second alternated every six pitches.

- At one point while leading, the guide chose not to insert a second ice screw into an anchor point (*regular and approved practice*) in order to save time while moving to a more sheltered position. He was concerned about rock falls, which he felt necessitated immediate avoiding action.

- A sheet of ice gave way under the client before he could move to the more sheltered position and he was swept away as the single ice screw came loose.

Judgment:

- It was held that the guide had abandoned accepted climbing procedure described as 'the universal law' in failing to provide a strong enough anchor/belay on the ice face by using only a single ice screw instead of two.

- The client was deemed to have consented to the ordinary risks of climbing but not to the risk of injury or death brought about by a breach of duty of care at the standard of a reasonably careful and competent alpine guide.

- The judge felt, on the evidence given, that there was no immediate risk of a rock fall and it was even more remote that the client would be hit in the short time it would have taken to follow regular and approved practice by inserting a second ice screw. The guide was judged to have had the time to 'make a calm assessment of the situation'.

Issues to consider:

- *Regular and approved practice* should be followed.

- In an emergency, the person in charge should balance the risks involved with the options that are available.

- Those deemed to be *specialists* should have a greater insight into the implications of their actions. Thus, they will be judged at a higher level of responsibility.

- Risk assessment and contingency planning are essential to the preparation of adventure activities.

- The practice of short cuts should be avoided.

Case 77

Activity: Dance
Age: Adult
Principle: Adequate warm-up

HILL v DURHAM COUNTY COUNCIL
Court of Appeal, 2000
Zurich Municipal *Court Circular*, May 2000

Summary:

- A 51-year-old teacher participated in a dance lesson during a professional development day.

- Part of the warm-up involved hopscotch, during which the teacher ruptured a tendon.

- The claimant argued that there should have been a gentler and more progressive warm-up routine before such vigorous activity.

- The claimant stated that no enquiries were made about her fitness beforehand.

Judgment:

- The Court of Appeal dismissed the claim.

- The judgment held that warm-up exercises can never rule out possible injury and that the way in which the injury was sustained was not foreseeable.

Issues to consider:

- It is good practice to enquire after the fitness of the individuals in the group, before moving on to a demanding activity in order to forewarn them of the demands of the particular activity.

- The context of the warm-up should be related to the forthcoming activity. Bizarre and hazardous activities where the benefit is not clearly apparent may result in a successful claim for damages.

Case 78

Activity: Gymnastics
Age: Secondary
Principle: Warm-up activities

A (a minor) v LEEDS CITY COUNCIL
Leeds County Court, 1999
Zurich Municipal *Court Circular*, September 1999

Summary:

- An 11-year-old girl was injured during a physical education lesson.

- The class of 25 pupils was told to run and touch all four corners of the gymnasium before returning to the teacher.

- The girl was injured in a collision as the pupils criss-crossed on different paths of travel.

Judgment:

- The claim for damages was upheld.

- The judge determined that the teacher was not in control of the exercise as she was unable to stop a collision once everyone had set off.

- 'There was no order and sequence to the exercise and a collision was entirely foreseeable.'

Issues to consider:

- This decision may disturb some school staff in that, under normal circumstances, the judgment that the teacher could not stop a collision once everyone had set off could apply to many activities they supervise. In practice, such an assumption does not apply.

- The responsible adult should ensure that pupils:

  - do not run at speed in confined areas/bottlenecks

  - are under control when running so they are able to stop or change direction in order to avoid collisions, particularly before being placed in any competitive situation.

- The purpose of the activity should be clear and any possibility of the activity causing injury anticipated.

- The responsible adult must feel confident that the group has the ability to stop on command.

Case 79

Activity: Gymnastics
Age: Secondary
Principle: Insufficient supervision

COOKE v KENT COUNTY COUNCIL
King's Bench Division, 1949
1 Lloyd's Report 823
Lexis

Summary:

- A 15-year-old boy was injured during a game of *horses and jockeys* in a physical education lesson. This took place in 1947.

- After routine exercises 'by way of a diversion before going on to further stereotyped exercises', the teacher set up the game.

- In *horses and jockeys*, one boy sits on the back of another, upright boy. In this *piggy-back* position, they try to unhorse others by pulling or pushing them.

- The groups were paired off, told to mount and then to start. Justice Harman said, 'Being a trained man, as he is, he would not have started any game in a physical training class without some such order'. The judge did not accept the pupil's version that they started without any instruction, the basis of the claim being one of inadequate supervision.

- A minute or so into the game the claimant slipped, falling to the ground with his partner on top of him. He broke his arm, causing permanent loss of flexibility.

- An initial claim that this was 'a game that was risky in itself, a dangerous game and involved the risk of injury', was dropped because of the judgment of an earlier case (*Jones v London County Council*, 96 JP 371).

Judgment:

- The incident (and the claim) was dismissed as 'a very unlucky accident'. Remember that the standard of care has increased significantly since 1947.

- The *Jones v London County Council* decision indicated that the judgment in this case should rest on the fact that 'this was not a game properly played'.

- It was decided that, as the injury occurred so early in the game, the boys would only be beginning to get excited and thus any roughness would be minimal. Justice Harman said, 'Unless there is some loss of temper, I cannot see that the game could be called rough. There was no discrepancy in age or strength...to make any grading off or special pairing either necessary or desirable'.

- It was accepted that the teacher was looking in the other direction. However, it was held that:

  His duty cannot be greater than that of a careful father. With a family of this size under his eye he cannot look everywhere at once. The fact that he was not looking at the moment was not a contributory cause of the accident.

- This comparison with the careful parent test contrasts the decision with that of the more recent case of *Porter v London Borough of Barking and Dagenham* (Case 2, page 68).

- Justice Harman also said, 'It does seem to me that the notion which has grown up that whenever anybody suffers injury he must necessarily be able to get compensation from somebody else must not be encouraged'.

Issues to consider:

- It is extremely unlikely that the judgment stating that the game was an acceptable activity would be the same today. It is foreseeable that pulling and pushing could cause injury.

- The idiosyncratic views of the judge at that time are evident.

- The judge's comments about school staff having responsibility for large groups and thus not being able to see everything at once is helpful to school staff, as is the final comment quoted above. Good positioning to enable the responsible adult to view the whole class, observation and analysis of what is happening plus appropriate intervention, if deemed to be necessary, are crucial.

- Clear organisation and control within contact activities are important, as is the need to group individuals according to size, strength, experience and confidence.

Case 80

Activity: Gymnastics
Age: Secondary
Principle: Medical background and parental communication

MOORE *v* HAMPSHIRE COUNTY COUNCIL
Court of Appeal, 1981
80 LGR 481 *The Times*, **6 November 1981, 8001336 Transcript Association**
Lexis

Summary:

- A 12-year-old girl who was born with dislocated hips had several operations, resulting in an artificial hip joint and a permanent limp.

- The girl's mother very carefully and repeatedly informed each school that her daughter attended that she was not to participate in physical education and games.

- The head teacher informed the physical education teacher that the girl was not to participate.

- The girl was desperately keen to join in. She sowed the seeds over time and hoped that she would soon be given permission. Eventually, she took her kit.

- She told the teacher that she was allowed to join in and the teacher accepted her word.

- During a paired activity that involved working on handstands, the girl fell and broke her ankle. She was off school for three months. The teacher had not supervised closely.

- A charge of negligence was brought.

Judgment:

- The claim was dismissed in the first instance and reversed at appeal.

- The appeal judges highlighted two issues:

  - The teacher ignored a directive from the head teacher without checking back or receiving alternative instructions about the participation of the girl.

  - The teacher failed to keep a close watch on the girl when setting quite a difficult task in what was the girl's first gymnastics lesson. She failed to cater for the girl's individual needs and background.

- Justice Watkins said:

  I would hold that there was no supervision of the girl whatsoever. In many cases of this nature, the question is not whether there was supervision at all but whether there was reasonable supervision having regard to the kind of physical activity going on. But here this schoolmistress did not observe this girl even begin a movement of which any reasonable person seeing it would have said: 'This won't do; it is not safe for a girl who limps and has been prohibited from taking part'.

Issues to consider:

- Activities should be within the known capabilities and experience of the pupils involved.

- Notes from parents remain active until:
  - cancelled by a further and more recent note
  - directly instructed otherwise by the head teacher, who has been notified of the details.

- If a responsible adult is suspicious of the authenticity of a parental note, the request made in the note should be followed regardless. The issue of authenticity should then be investigated after the lesson.

- It is important to check pupil medical records to ensure that pupils' fitness is at an adequate level in order to enable them to participate in particular activities.

- Long-term non-participants should be closely monitored when they initially rejoin lessons.

- Tasks may need to be adjusted for some pupils if their previous performance has been prejudiced by absence or injury.

5.6 CASES OF NEGLIGENCE RELATING TO ACTIVITY ORGANISATION: TEACHING AND ORGANISATION

Case 81

Activity: Athletics
Age: Secondary
Principle: Ensuring the safety of pupils

DARBY (a minor) v WORCESTERSHIRE COUNTY COUNCIL 2003
Wragge and Company News and Views **January 2004**

Summary:

- An 11-year-old pupil was injured while performing a standing long jump during an indoor athletics session.

- The boy fell backwards, sustaining a fractured arm.

- He alleged that the injury arose from the lack of supervision. There was only one teacher to supervise a class of 30 pupils.

- The teacher stated that he had tutored the pupils on how to perform the task and forewarned them to have their feet away from the edge of the mat on which they were landing, in order to avoid catching their feet and injuring themselves. Other pupils supported this claim.

- The pupil claimed not to have heard the teacher when the tuition had taken place. He argued that he had not been told that, if he took off too close to the mat, there was a risk of catching his foot and hurting himself.

Judgment:

- The judge supported the boy's claim.

- He found that, although satisfied that the teacher in question had given the pupils a demonstration in how to perform the task, he had not 'drummed home' that the reason they should take off away from the edge of the mat was that they could trip and be injured.

- Contributory negligence was not considered.

Issues to consider:

- As this decision came from the County Court, it is considered to be a 'persuasive' judgment, rather than a judgment that sets a precedent.

- This is considered to be a very harsh decision within the legal profession.

- This judgment indicates the need to teach pupils technique and to provide clear reasons why pupils have been taught to perform these techniques and skills in particular ways. There is also a need to explain the hazard in not doing an activity as taught.

Case 82

Activity: Gaelic football
Age: Secondary
Principle: Comparable size when participating in games

> ### WARD *v* DONEGAL VOCATIONAL EDUCATION COMMITTEE 1994
> ### Irish Law Times 103 (Ireland)
> ### Zurich Municipal *Court Circular*

Summary:

- A schoolboy was injured during a game of Gaelic football.

- He argued that the school should not have mixed taller boys with those of a lesser stature in a contact sport.

- He also argued that the school had been in breach of its duty of care to ensure that he was reasonably safe while playing the game.

Judgment:

- The case was dismissed. The judge rejected the argument that school teams must always be chosen so that players would not get hurt, because injury is an accepted hazard in physical contact sports.

- The game was judged to have been properly supervised by an experienced referee and two other teachers on the touchline.

Issues to consider:

- Schools are required to provide proper supervision of potentially harmful situations and to take sensible precautions.

- Games have evolved over time in order to accommodate players of different sizes.

- In representative matches, players are expected to have been taught the appropriate techniques. They should also be confident in their application against opponents, regardless of size.

- In teaching situations, it may be prudent to match size, experience, strength, skill and confidence in contact or weight-bearing situations, or where an accelerating projectile is involved.

Case 83

Activity: Golf
Age: Adult
Principle: Awareness of others in the work area

HORTON v JACKSON
Court of Appeal, 1996
John Larking
Lexis

Summary:

- A golfer was struck on the head by a ball driven from an adjacent tee. He lost an eye. There were clear instructions within the club rules requiring those on the tee to wait until the adjacent area was clear.

- Both the golfer striking the ball and the club were sued for injury under the Occupiers' Liability Act 1957.

- The arrangement of the course was very tight.

- The golfer teeing off did not look to see if the way was clear. This part of the course was widely known to be hazardous.

- The club only introduced an accident book in 1990 and this had not been appropriately completed over that time.

Judgment:

- The claimant was not found to have contributed to any negligence.

- In the first instance, the golfer striking the ball was judged to be negligent but the club was not.

- At appeal, it was revealed that there was a limited history of injuries at the hole and the club had not posted warning notices or redesigned that part of the course. These were not deemed to have affected the incident. The club was not deemed responsible.

Issues to consider:

- Good positioning to enable the responsible adult to view the whole class, observation and analysis of what is happening plus appropriate intervention, if deemed to be necessary, are crucial.

- When working in a confined space, pupils should be taught to check the area into which they are about to propel any ball or other item before doing so.

- Pupils should have reasonable expectations of striking the ball accurately.

- The use of warning notices in confined spaces can be reasonably expected.

- More recent case law indicates that judgments have gone against the person striking the ball without a reasonable level of control.

Case 84

Activity: Gymnastics
Age: Primary
Principle: Progressive practices and prior experience

COTTON v KENT COUNTY COUNCIL
Queen's Bench Division, 1983
81/NJ/4503 Barnet Lenton
Lexis

Summary:

- In a gymnastics class of 33 pupils aged between eight and nine, a pupil was injured while doing a side vault. She had not vaulted before and the teacher was some distance from the piece of apparatus.

- A springboard was positioned by a bar box.

- The teacher had demonstrated how to use the springboard and some vaults but had not taught them to the class. He had told the class not to attempt anything they did not feel confident that they could do.

- During the court hearing, the teacher's recollection was inconsistent with information on the accident report form. The detail on the form that had been completed at the time of the injury was scant, for example, the teacher could not recall talking with a non-participating pupil when the accident happened.

Judgment:

- Negligence by the teacher was found on the basis of the following:
  - The class had seen the springboard and box but had not been taught how to use them for vaulting.
  - The teacher had not made it sufficiently clear to the class not to vault unless there was help.
  - The teacher was talking to a non-participating pupil with his back to the class for some time when the accident occurred and thus failed to notice that some children were vaulting rather than climbing onto the box.
  - The injured pupil was trying to perform an action that was held to be 'too difficult for her in light of her experience and capacity'.
  - The teacher failed to remove the springboard in order to prevent vaulting. Judge Webster said:

    The springboard constituted an invitation to children to use it in order to try to jump or vault over the box and...if those children, at that age, used the springboard for attempting to jump or vault the box, it was reasonably to be contemplated that some child might need assistance if injury was to be avoided and that would be all the more to be contemplated if they had not been trained in the use of the springboard. A child of that age cannot be expected to be fully aware of the extent of his own ability.

- Contributory negligence by the pupil was dismissed on the grounds that 'she tried to do a little bit more that she was capable of and, at that age, that does not constitute contributory negligence'. However, it was acknowledged that it might have been very different if the springboard had been moved into place by the pupils when it had been put out of use by the teacher.

Issues to consider:

- The judge's suggestion that a child aged between eight and nine years cannot be expected to be fully aware of the extent of their own abilities indicates an expectation for adults to:
  - use carefully staged progressive practices
  - be vigilant in observation
  - communicate clearly with pupils regarding what they may or may not do.

- If clear warnings are given to a class, the adult may be absolved from liability. However, this depends on the age of the class and whether or not the class is known to be well behaved. Where warnings are given, they should be specific to the dangers involved in the particular activity.

- It is advisable to have a school policy to complete accident report forms fully and to record detailed, supplementary information, using diagrams, which should be filed centrally in school.

- Springboards are not usual pieces of equipment for primary school gymnastics lessons. Such rebound equipment, if used, should be carefully introduced and managed.

- Risk assessments are mandatory and should highlight potential hazards at the planning stage.

- As established in an early case (*Barfoot v East Sussex DC 1939,* Case 3, page 69), it is incumbent upon school staff to highlight risks and warn against them.

- Activities should be within the known capabilities and experience of the pupils involved. This may involve prohibiting certain equipment or skills.

- Responsible adults should be aware of class management issues when controlling prescribed gymnastic movements, as opposed to creative gymnastic movements. The whole issue of standing by and supporting becomes very important – details of this can be found in *Safe Practice in Physical Education and School Sport* (baalpe, 2004)[1].

[1] British Association of Advisers and Lecturers in Physical Education (baalpe). (2004) *Safe Practice in Physical Education and School Sport.* Leeds: Coachwise Solutions. ISBN: 1 902523 68 7.

Case 85

Activity: Gymnastics
Age: Primary
Principle: Inadequate supervision and prior experience

JONES v HAMPSHIRE COUNTY COUNCIL
Court of Appeal (Civil Division), 1997
Transcript: Smith Bernal
Lexis

Summary:

- Action was brought by the claimant 13 years after the incident.

- The pupil was 11 years old when the incident occurred. He was participating in a gymnastics lesson in 1983.

- A group was using a vaulting table, which had been introduced to the school between approximately three and four weeks before the incident occurred.

- The class had not used the equipment before in the way in which they were using it during that particular lesson.

- It was alleged that 'they were not told precisely what to do with it'. The claimant alleged that no task had been set.

- Another pupil performed forward rolls along the table and the claimant copied.

- Two rolls along the table were performed successfully but she fell awkwardly during the third roll and broke her arm.

- The pupil alleged inadequate instruction, inadequate supervision and an unsafe system being used by the teacher. 'This was an exercise she and the others with her should not have been allowed to perform, having regard to their age and limited skills, without immediate supervision.'

Judgment:

- In the first instance, negligence was held to be proven.

- The Court of Appeal said that 'it may be perfectly reasonable for a teacher to allow children to engage in an activity which, on the face of it, is fraught with danger if that teacher has made an assessment of those children and come to the conclusion that the activity is reasonably safe for them'.

- On the evidence provided, no such judgement had been made. The pupils were 'simply left to get on with it'.

- It was upheld by the Court of Appeal that 'the defendants did not do that which was required of them, namely, through their teacher, to apply an experienced eye to what was going on and decide whether or not it was an activity which was suitable for these children'.

- It was also held that:

  It is easy to draw the inference that the activity was, on the face of it, beyond the competence of this particular plaintiff [claimant]. It was up to the teacher to make sure that what they were doing was an activity they could properly undertake in safety, bearing in mind that the teacher could not be everywhere at once and could not necessarily be there to safeguard each child as he or she undertook a particular manoeuvre.

- A breach of duty was evident. The teacher should have seen that the particular activity was beyond the competence of this particular pupil.

Issues to consider:

- Cases may come to court several years after an incident.

- Pupils need to be psychologically prepared and confident of success when performing tasks.

- When carrying out general open-ended tasks, school staff/coaches are advised to:
  - regularly scan the class as it works
  - judge whether individuals appear to be confident and competent in their movement
  - focus individual responses that are observed within the experience and confidence of specific pupils
  - forewarn pupils of any potentially hazardous use.

- Classes should be introduced to new items of equipment and instructed how they may be used within the context of the work being undertaken.

- Specific skills should be tailored to individuals' needs, experience and confidence.

- In such situations, it is advisable to gather the class round to discuss the correct techniques and demonstrate the salient points, in order to consolidate understanding of the requirements to ensure safe performance.

Case 86

Activity: Gymnastics
Age: Secondary
Principle: Inappropriate progression

HEFFER v WILTSHIRE COUNTY COUNCIL
Devizes County Court, 1996

Summary:

- A 13-year-old boy was injured in a gymnastics lesson.

- Appropriate progressive practices leading to the straddle vault had been taught.

- Support was provided initially but withdrawn when appropriate. The injured boy was supported throughout the early stages and the teacher invited pupils to call for support if needed when progressing from a leapfrog to the buck.

- The pupil refused on his first vault over the buck. He lost his nerve but the teacher did not see this. The pupil was successful on his second attempt. However, from a one-foot take-off, the swing of his leg dislodged the supporting arm. He fell to the floor, injuring himself because he vaulted without support.

Judgment:

- Reference was made in court to baalpe's *Safe Practice in Physical Education and School Sport* regarding:
    - The assessment of mental and physical readiness before a new skill is taught.
    - If the pattern of movement is predictable, the teacher must be ready to stand by and give support throughout.

- The teacher was held to be negligent on the following basis:
    - The boy was supported during the leapfrog activity, so support should not have been withdrawn on the buck.
    - It should not have been left to the boy to *opt in* for support. Peer group pressure may prevent opting in and a reduction in support was deemed to be premature and total rather than gradual.
    - The teacher acknowledged that a one-foot take-off indicated a lack of full control or confidence. He could not respond positively when pressed as to why he therefore had not provided support.

- It was held that progression to the buck was a new activity and that support was thus mandatory.

Issues to consider:

- It is becoming increasingly common to establish systems of *opting out* of support rather than *opting in* to it, in order to ensure no misunderstandings and that pupils have the confidence to perform the task.

- Pupils should be psychologically prepared and confident of success when performing tasks.

- It should be considered whether it is wise for pupils receiving support on one task to progress to another related task without support.

- It was an idiosyncratic opinion of the judge that vaulting over a buck was a 'new skill' rather than a progression.

Case 87

Activity: Gymnastics
Age: Secondary
Principle: Need for support

POVEY v GOVERNORS OF RYDAL SCHOOL
Manchester Adjourned Winter Assizes, 1969
(1970) 1 ALL ER 841
Lexis

Summary:

- A 16-year-old pupil fell and was seriously injured while dismounting from an Olympic rings activity in a school gymnasium. As a result, he became quadriplegic (all four limbs are paralysed).

- The pupil had performed the rings exercise over a period of two years.

- As he executed the *straddle off* (legs astride the hands and rings, loosening the grip so as to dismount to the floor from a height of over 2 m) he fell onto his shoulders and neck.

Judgment:

- The governors and physical education teacher were found to be negligent.

- It was held that the particular exercise was within the capabilities of the pupil and that the teacher was competent enough to teach it.

- Liability was found on the following basis:
  - The landing mat used was a tumbling mat and, according to Justice Crichton, was inappropriate to 'provide sufficient protection against injury caused through a fall and this constituted a breach of duty'.
  - The pupil had not been warned about the necessity of having an adequate warm-up or that an insufficient warm-up might have contributed to the accident.
  - A *stand-in* should have been provided to minimise the risk of injury from a fall. Failure to provide for this and to impress its importance on the claimant was a breach of duty.

Issues to consider:

- Teachers and coaches of specialist forms of gymnastics should be appropriately qualified or trained.

- Mats should be appropriate to the activity taking place. Deep, soft, weight-absorbent mattresses are necessary where unpredicted and poorly coordinated landings or falls may occur when the body is travelling at speed. Conversely, these would be inappropriate for landing from simple vaults. Here, one inch deep, tumbling mats are more appropriate.

- Adequate warm-up and cool-down activities are particularly vital in high-level gymnastics. While scientific research is divided on the benefits of warm-up/cool-down, the possible benefit of warm-up on performance has been accepted by the courts.

- Responsible adults should think very carefully about whether supports or *stand-ins* are necessary. This tends to occur when movements are set and thus predictable, as in formal gymnastic skills rather than free movement planned by the performer. When a support or *stand-in* is available, very clear communication is necessary between the adult and the performer in order to ensure that no misunderstandings arise. The *stand-in* should be fully trained in the correct supporting techniques and should display a responsible attitude to the job.

Case 88

Activity: Gymnastics
Age: Secondary
Principle: Adequate supervision

GLEAVE *v* LANCASHIRE COUNTY COUNCIL
1951
Croner, pp 3–463

Summary:

- A girl vaulted over a buck and fell and injured herself.

- The teacher had monitored the girl's progress and decided that the girl could perform the activity without support.

Judgment:

- Damages were awarded.

- The judge agreed that the teacher had properly decided that the girl was capable of performing the task without support but, on the evidence given, it was held that the girl was at the stage where shadow supporting was needed in case she stumbled.

- It was determined that the teacher, in this instance, should have been standing by the mat, as near as possible to the line of vault and close enough to be able to hold the girl if she stumbled.

Issues to consider:

- Even today, the principle applies to:
  - supporting pupils who are not very proficient
  - standing by when proficiency develops in case the pupil stumbles on landing
  - there being no need to stand by when the pupil has become proficient.

- It is becoming increasingly common to establish systems of *opting out* of support rather than *opting in* to it, in order to ensure no misunderstandings and that pupils have the confidence to perform the task.

Case 89

Activity: Gymnastics
Age: Secondary
Principle: Special care in the use of apparatus

KERSHAW v HAMPSHIRE COUNTY COUNCIL
1982
Croner, pp 3:460

Summary:

- A 12-year-old girl was injured when using a trampette to vault over a box.

- She fell when the rebound from the trampette caused her to go too high and too fast.

- She had participated successfully in the activity.

- Two pupils were acting as catchers.

- The teacher left the gymnasium to go to the office prior to the girl's injury.

Judgment:

- It was held that it should have been known that the use of a trampette presented a higher risk than a normal springboard.

- The teacher should have been present to provide the necessary support and supervision throughout this particular exercise.

- If the teacher had to leave the pupils, the lesson should have been stopped.

Issues to consider:

- The law does not require pupils to be supervised every minute of the day but effective supervision is essential.

- Close supervision is required of activities using rebound apparatus, such as trampolines or trampettes.

- Pupils in support/catching capacities should be taught effectively, monitored regularly and matched according to physique and strength.

- Only in extreme circumstances should the responsible adult leave the class. No activity should be allowed while they are absent.

Case 90

Activity: Gymnastics
Age: Secondary
Principle: Safe systems

OGDEN v ROTHERHAM MBC
Barnsley County Court, 16 April 1997

Summary:

- The 14-year-old claimant was injured doing a through vault over a beam saddle.

- The claimant had not performed the vault before.

- Two teachers were present. This was disputed by the claimant but reinforced by others in the lesson.

- Each teacher was positioned to support the pupils on landing.

- The teacher involved spoke to the claimant but what was said was disputed.

- The claimant approached the vault and grasped the handles, but did not tuck up his legs as he vaulted. As his legs hit the beam saddle, he over-balanced and released his grip with one hand, causing him to twist. He was caught by the teacher but the twist and momentum caused him to fracture his arm.

Judgment:

- The judge said, 'Everyone accepts there will be risks. The school's responsibility is to provide a safe system thereby reducing the likelihood of injury'.

- 'A safe system means:
  - explanation by the teacher of the lesson
  - demonstration
  - relevant warm-up
  - teacher(s) standing in to assist
  - ensuring that the pupil has a high expectation of completing the task successfully.'

- The judge dismissed the claim on the basis that a safe system existed, particularly with two members of staff present and the teacher being in a position to provide support. The outcome was not foreseeable.

Issues to consider:

- The safe system described by the judge is very particular. Teachers should think through what is to take place in the lesson and establish appropriate guidance, support and progression.

- It is advisable to establish a system where approved pupils may choose to work without support.

Case 91

Activity: Hockey
Age: Secondary
Principle: Personal protection

> **G (a child) v LANCASHIRE COUNTY COURT**
> **Burnley County Court, 2000**
> **3 QR12 2001**
> **O-Pro Group**

Summary:

- A 14-year-old girl received an accidental blow to her mouth from a hockey stick while playing on a grass pitch.

- She lost six teeth and suffered severe bruising and lacerations to her lip.

- The injured girl had not played much hockey. The player who hit the ball and followed through with her stick played for the school team.

- The claimant alleged that there had been inadequate teaching of stick work and tackling technique in the lessons, neither had there been any insistence on the use of a mouthguard nor explanation of the benefits of using one.

- The LEA defended the claim, stating that adequate teaching had taken place and that the claimant was injured because she had gone into the tackle too low as opposed to the opponent having her hockey stick too high.

- The LEA admitted that the pupils had been told about the benefit of wearing mouthguards but nothing had been communicated to the parents.

- No national guidelines exist, although *Safe Practice in Physical Education* (baalpe, 2004)[1] states that:

  Protective devices (eg mouthguards, body armour for goal keepers in hockey, helmets for batters and close fielders in cricket) enable wearers to take part in physical activity by reducing high risk to reasonable risk. Although not compulsory, it is good practice for pupils to wear mouthguards to protect their teeth and gums in invasion games such as rugby, hockey and lacrosse.

  Whenever possible, they should be properly modelled and fitted by a dental practitioner. Off-the-shelf mouthguards may not provide the same level of protection. Parents should be informed about issues relating to the wearing of mouthguards during games activities.

[1] British Association of Advisers and Lecturers in Physical Education (baalpe). (2004) *Safe Practice in Physical Education and School Sport.* Leeds: Coachwise Solutions. ISBN: 1 902523 68 7.

Judgment:

- The judge asked the two parties to try to come to some agreement without the case being fought in court. After discussion, an order was agreed by consent between the claimant and defendant. The injured girl was awarded compensation for pain and future dental treatment.

- When commenting on the claim, the judge rejected the view that the girl's mother should take responsibility without having been given advice by the school or LEA. He also criticised the statement that the girls had been 'told in passing during the first lesson something which looks fairly vague, but nothing was done to tell the parents about it'.

Issues to consider:

- Mandatory requirements to wear mouthguards at junior international level to county level are set out by national governing bodies for sports such as rugby and lacrosse. Other national governing bodies advise such precautions.

- It is essential that parents are sent written information informing them that mouthguards are either mandatory or advisable for participation in games. Simply telling the pupils is clearly insufficient.

- Each school should have a written policy about the use of mouthguards and other personal protection and should ensure that it is applied consistently.

- In some schools, a mandatory requirement for mouthguards will have little affect on levels of pupil participation. However, in others it will decimate participation if the cost for individually fitted protection is too high for families to afford. *Boil and bite* mouthguards can cost as little as a few pence, may be *re-boiled* and *refitted* as the pupil grows, and certainly provide better protection than no mouthguard at all. Individually fitted mouthguards provide the best protection as they are thicker and spread the force of a blow more widely. However, these are much more expensive.

- Schools may establish mandatory or advisory policies on the wearing of mouthguards. In either instance, parents should be fully informed of the implications. It falls to the adult in charge of an activity to ensure that the situation remains safe for those taking part. Where mandatory, allowing pupils to participate without a mouthguard is in breach of the policy. Where advisory, it remains the responsibility of the adult in charge to ensure that the activity is safe and that the likelihood of injury is minimal for pupils without mouthguards. This may mean adjusting the activity to minimise such likelihood. The correct methods of teaching technical skills, and adequate supervision to avoid overly boisterous play, are also essential.

- Where parents provide such personal protection, schools need to ensure that changes to the curriculum at short notice do not place pupils at risk of injury because they have not brought the appropriate items of personal protection to school with them.

- Any willingness on the part of parents to indemnify school staff should be ignored. Indemnities have no legal status as pupils may bring retrospective action within three years of reaching adult age.

Case 92

Activity: Physical education
Age: Primary
Principle: Wearing jewellery

**R v THE CHAIR and GOVERNORS OF CWNFELINFACH PRIMARY SCHOOL
(EX PARTE ROBERTS)
High Court, London, 2001
Daily Mail, 8 and 23 March 2001**

Summary:

- A seven-year-old girl was excluded from physical education lessons, club activities and playtime activities by her school because her parents insisted, to prevent infection, that she did not remove her earrings. The school determined that wearing earrings and studs in activity sessions was a safety hazard.

- The parents brought the action under the Human Rights Act 1998, alleging victimisation and unlawfully depriving the girl of full access to the National Curriculum.

- When the girl wore earrings to school an alternative, non-hazardous occupation was organised.

- The school argued that the ban on wearing jewellery in physical education lessons was lawful and appropriate for reasons of health and safety.

Judgment:

- The judge initially asked the parents and school to try to reach a compromise but this was not achieved.

- The judge then ruled that the school was entitled to exclude the girl on the basis of health and safety.

- A claim that the exclusion breached the European Convention on Human Rights was rejected.

Issues to consider:

- The wearing of jewellery poses a foreseeable hazard to individuals or others around them in physical education and school sport. This decision clarifies the responsibility of school staff in this area.

- In order to minimise the potential of jewellery to be a foreseeable hazard in physical activity, the following steps should be taken:
  - All jewellery should be removed.
  - If the jewellery cannot be removed, the situation should be made safe, for example, by adjusting the activity for the individual or group.
  - If the situation cannot be made safe, the individual should not participate.
  - Body jewellery may be hidden. Pupils should be asked at the beginning of lessons if they are wearing body jewellery. If disclosed, the previous principles should be applied. If there are no admissions, the lesson may proceed as planned. If teachers become aware of any body jewellery being worn during the lesson, they should apply the above principles as soon as they become aware of the situation.

- Taping over studs is sometimes used as a strategy to make the situation safe. Such practice:
  - may not be effective if the individual's ear could potentially be struck forcibly by a ball or flailing arm
  - requires a clear decision to be made regarding who applies and removes the tape (ie the staff, pupil or other adult)
  - is subject to the fact that the supervising adult remains responsible for the effectiveness of the strategy, regardless of who applies the tape.

- Any willingness on the part of parents to indemnify school staff should be ignored. Indemnities have no legal status as pupils may bring retrospective action within three years of reaching adult age.

Case 93

Activity: Rugby
Age: Secondary
Principle: Pupil personal accident insurance and the importance of teaching techniques

---

VAN OPPEN v CLERK TO THE BEDFORD CHARITY TRUSTEES
Queen's Bench Division, 1988
1 All ER 273
Lexis

Summary:

- A pupil was seriously injured when he tackled an opponent during a school rugby match. This resulted in incomplete quadriplegia (incomplete paralysis of all four limbs) and some recovery has occurred.

- The pupil sued the school alleging negligence in failing to:
  - coach or instruct in proper tackling techniques
  - insure the pupil against accidental injury
  - advise parents of the risk of serious injury in rugby, of the need for personal accident insurance or of the fact that the school had not arranged such insurance.

Judgment:

- The claim was dismissed but it was recognised that the case broke new ground.

- It was held that the school was not negligent in its coaching of rugby in that the injury was accidental. It was the result of a mistimed tackle that arose from a flying tackle coinciding with the opponent checking his stride, which caused the tackler's head to crash into, rather than behind, the opponents hip. Justice Boreham said:

  His technique was correct. The tackle went wrong because the opponent was sufficiently skilful and agile to check his stride at the crucial moment. It was no more and no less than a tragic accident. The standard of supervision was high, the refereeing was vigilant and strict and...there was an emphasis on discipline, which meant playing the game correctly.

- It was held that the school had thoroughly investigated the issue of pupil personal injury insurance; had provided the parents with a factual account of the situation; had looked for leading advice from national governing bodies; and had accepted the school's policy of seeking to provide insurance for all pupils in all activities, rather than a voluntary scheme for rugby only by which, if two pupils were injured, one may be covered and the other not. It was further accepted that it was the school's duty to insure against negligence and it was the parents' responsibility to consider personal injury insurance.

The judge said:

> There is no general duty arising simply from the relationship of school and pupil
> to ensure that the plaintiff was insured against accidental injury [because]...there
> is no such duty on parents. If there is no such duty on parents...there can be no
> duty on those in loco parentis. The school's duty is more limited than that of the
> parents. It relates to matters over which the school has control and to no other
> matters. What is a matter of choice or discretion for the parent is outside the
> ambit of the duty of the school. If this duty were to be imposed, then we are
> getting very close to no fault liability.

- It was held that the school had no obligation to advise about the risk of injury (a
  situation somewhat contradictory to the later outcome of Case 91, page 256 or the
  need for personal accident insurance because parents are under no duty to act upon it.
  The judge further commented that a school's duty is simply to take care to protect the
  pupils from foreseeable harm and the law expects no more. However, the court did feel
  that 'it would have been prudent and careful so to advise the parents...but liability only
  arises when there is a legal duty not to be careless'.

Issues to consider:

- Pupils should not be required to participate in activities that are considered to carry an
  unacceptable risk of injury.

- Staff should carefully organise and supervise games and lessons, and must be strict
  and vigilant when refereeing.

- Pupils should be taught the necessary techniques, skills and rules to play games with
  reasonable safety, through experiencing appropriate, progressive practices.

- It is prudent to educate parents about personal injury insurance. The school should
  inform parents about the programme in which the pupils will participate, whether or not
  the school has taken out pupil personal injury insurance. If the school has pupil
  personal injury insurance, parents should be aware of the levels of insurance. Parents
  may then choose whether to take further action.

- Regardless of the nature and level of the programme, school staff are expected to only
  allow activities that reasonably suit the level of ability of each individual involved. The
  courts generally recognise that no activity is inherently unsafe in itself.

Case 94

Activity: Skiing
Age: Secondary
Principle: Ongoing risk assessment

C (a child) *v* **W SCHOOL**
Court of Appeal, 2002
Croner Special Report No 59
15 July 2002

Summary:

- The claimant was one of three senior boys who joined a skiing trip organised by his school. The trip was primarily for younger pupils.

- The three older pupils had varying levels of competence at skiing.

- The boys' parents signed consent forms allowing the three older boys to ski together unsupervised but to act within the established code of conduct for the school. The boys were under the control of the teachers for general supervision and behaviour but could ski separately.

- At the trial, the boys claimed to have doubts about the basic rules of skiing and whether the skier's code had been explained to them.

- The staff deemed the older boys sufficiently competent to ski alone and believed that their behaviour was satisfactory. None of the parents queried this assessment, neither was it criticised at trial.

- Incidents occurred that were not associated with the skiing which questioned the older boys' maturity, such as being caught smoking with younger boys. Disciplinary action was taken.

- Later in the holiday they were seen skiing off-piste, knowing that this was not allowed. A reasonable explanation caused the teacher not to take further action.

- Later in the week they deliberately skied off-piste, claiming that the teacher had given permission. The teacher denied this. A severe reprimand was given but no punishment was imposed. The teacher threatened to take away the boys' ski passes but did not do so.

- The following day, the boys again skied unsupervised on a run that was within their capabilities. One boy skied too fast and out of control. He failed to take heed of warning notices and to be aware of slower skiers. He fell, which resulted in a serious disability.

Judgment:

- No criticism was made of the planning of the trip.

- The judge at the original hearing held that the staff had a duty to take reasonable care of all the pupils.

- The decision to let the older boys ski alone was conditional upon them behaving in a mature and responsible way. The Court of Appeal added that this could include a duty to take positive steps by way of supervision or otherwise to protect the boys from harm.

- The first judge determined that the lapses in responsible behaviour by skiing off-piste required stronger discipline than a reprimand. 'In failing to impose substantial sanctions for this deliberate breach of instructions [the teacher] failed in the exercise of the duty of care he had undertaken.' The judge determined that taking the ski passes away or requiring the older boys to ski with the main group was more reasonable action to be expected.

- The judge at the original hearing found that irresponsibility was the primary cause of the accident and held that this would not have happened if the teacher had been more severe in his discipline. The teacher was found to be negligent in failing to react appropriately.

- Contributory negligence was assessed at fifty per cent, with damages reduced accordingly.

- The Court of Appeal essentially agreed with the facts but took a different view about the teacher's response to the second off-piste incident, deciding that the teacher chose an option within a reasonable range of measures. It was concluded that a reprimand was within that reasonable range of options and that the root cause of the injury was carelessness on the part of the boy, not disobedience.

- The Court of Appeal overturned the original decision that the school had been negligent.

Issues to consider:

- Off-site visits have a very important role to play in the overall education of young people.

- Duty of care is a process requiring ongoing assessments of risk according to the circumstances as this case emphasises. Good planning will do much to discharge a reasonable duty of care.

- The level of risk varies according to the activity and the challenge involved. This determines the level of planning necessary.

- Schools can demonstrate that all the issues have been considered in a documented risk assessment.

Case 95

Activity: Sports days
Age: Primary
Principle: Limits of supervision

SIMMONDS v ISLE OF WIGHT COUNCIL
London High Court, 2003
The *Guardian* and the *Daily Mail*, 25 September 2003

Summary:

- A five-year-old boy had a picnic with his parents on the school grounds prior to the start of the school sports day. He then left his parents to go to his teacher for the beginning of the event.

- On the way, he strayed onto a playground with swings. Pretending to be Superman, he jumped off the swing, fell and badly fractured his arm in three places.

- The school staff were aware of the hazard posed by the swings and had placed them out of bounds. The swings were not defective.

Judgment:

- The judge reversed the decision made at an earlier hearing in the County Court at which the school staff had been found negligent and damages had been awarded to the pupil. At the initial hearing, the judge determined that the school staff, aware of the hazard, should have immobilised the swings or taped them off.

- The appeal hearing reversed the initial decision, absolving the school of blame, and refused damages on the basis that playing fields cannot be freed from all hazards. It was held that the original decision lacked reality and common sense. The judge warned:

  If the payout had been allowed to stand it could have signalled the end of similar traditional public events. The probability is that sports days and other pleasurable sporting events will simply not take place. Such events could easily become uninsurable or only insurable at prohibitive cost. Playing fields cannot be made free from all hazards.

- The judge also determined that no amount of supervision by the teachers would have prevented the accident, believing that it was 'slightly unreal' to suggest that the school owed a legal duty to warn parents of the hazards of unsupervised play on swings.

- LEA representatives hailed the reversal as a victory for common sense against 'ambulance chasers'. The LEA appealed the initial judgment because of the dangerous precedent it might set. The boy's parents were required to repay the award and substantial costs.

Issues to consider:

- School staff should make parents aware of when their children are the responsibility of the parents and when the staff assume responsibility for an organised event.

- Forewarning children and parents of hazards on the school site is important.

Case 96

Activity: Tennis
Age: Primary
Principle: Inadequate supervision and control

BELL v STAFFORDSHIRE COUNTY COUNCIL
Stoke on Trent County Court, 2003
Zurich Municipal *Court Circular*, December 2003

Summary:

- An eight-year-old girl suffered a nasty eye injury when struck by a tennis ball during a school break.

- An experienced teacher was nearby on playground duty. Of the 70 pupils in the area, approximately 30 were involved in sporting activities on the playground.

- A third of the area was allocated to football, another third to tennis and the middle third to people walking in and out.

- A group of boys playing tennis had turned their playing area at an angle to that of the girls, so that the balls were hit towards the girls' court.

- The girls were using plastic rackets whereas the boys were playing with strung rackets, which propelled the ball faster.

- One of the boys was described as 'silly' as he was hitting the ball hard and in a careless way. He had allegedly been told not to hit the ball so fiercely.

Judgment:

- The court accepted that the school was well run but the council was found liable for inadequate supervision and control, taking into account school life and the number and nature of the children.

- It was held that:
  - the boys playing tennis ought to have been playing in the same direction as the girls
  - the games were too close in proximity
  - the boys' rackets were powerful enough to make such an accident foreseeable.

- 'A reasonably careful supervising parent would at least have ensured that the games were conducted in the same direction as each other.'

Issues to consider:

- Initial organisation to provide a safe working environment needs to be regularly monitored to ensure that it remains safe.

- Games areas should be organised to ensure that *run-off* areas and accelerating projectiles (or, in this case, fiercely driven strokes) do not create a likelihood of injury for others working on, and focused on, other playing areas.

- The implications of using differentiated equipment should be considered within the overall organisation of a group, in order to ensure a safe working environment.

Case 97

Activity: Trampolining
Age: Primary
Principle: Inadequate footwear

VILLELLA v NORTH BEDFORDSHIRE BOROUGH COUNCIL
Queen's Bench Division, 1983
Transcript: Barnett, Lenton
Lexis

Summary:

- A nine-year-old girl broke her leg while trampolining at a local leisure centre. She caught her foot in the webbing of the bed, losing concentration and balance. This caused her to collapse and fracture her femur. She was barefooted.

- The girl had not been told to wear anything on her feet and none of the group had been corrected on this when taking their turns. Nothing had even been said about the need for some form of footwear during the two years during which some of the group had been attending the class.

- The injury occurred during the second turn of the evening.

- She had been to the centre several times before.

- The leisure centre staff argued that the injury was due to a bad bounce.

- The person responsible for the group was a qualified British Trampoline Federation (BTF) coach with approximately eight years' coaching experience. She had always trampolined in bare feet.

- The coach was standing by the trampoline, fully involved in the session.

Judgment:

- The claim was upheld. It was foreseeable that a toe could become entrapped in a web and the risk was heightened by the young age of the performer and subsequent size of her toe.

- The judge made it clear that it was not 'a wide and all embracing duty. Experienced performers may well prefer to perform in bare feet and may feel safer in doing so...but with this particular type of [claimant] there was a foreseeable and known risk'.

- The judge did not feel that the coach needed to be standing on the trampoline to assist the performer due to her previous experience and the low level demand of the activity. 'The coach's duty of care did not extend to standing on the trampoline itself.'

Issues to consider:

- The competence of a performer in a specific task should determine whether the coach is situated on the trampoline itself, or standing alongside it.

- As well as clothing and footwear, the absence of sharp objects such as buckles should be checked. Long hair should be tied back and other safety issues should be considered before allowing anyone to participate.

- Responsible adults should become familiar with any national governing body or other professional advice such as *Safe Practice in Physical Education and School Sport* (baalpe, 2004)[1] and apply the relevant guidance.

- It should be insisted that all performers wear non-slip socks or trampoline slippers when using the trampoline.

- Checking pupil understanding at each stage of the correct and safe mechanics of any skill or part-skill is important.

[1] British Association of Advisers and Lecturers in Physical Education (baalpe) (2004) *Safe Practice in Physical Education and School Sport*. Leeds: Coachwise Solutions. ISBN: 1 902523 68 7.

Case 98

Activity: Trampolining
Age: Secondary
Principle: Inappropriate progression

KENYON v LANCASHIRE COUNTY COUNCIL
Oldham County Court, 2001

Summary:

- A Year-11 pupil was injured while performing a backdrop in a trampolining lesson.

- She was reasonably experienced in the activity. Capable of performing all the basic feet-to-feet skills individually and in sequence, she was thus ready to learn a backdrop.

- The pupil was taken through the recognised progressive stages leading to the backdrop, including assistance by the teachers and the use of a safety mattress on the trampoline bed.

- The teacher was qualified and experienced in teaching trampolining.

- A wedge fracture injury was sustained to a lumbar vertebra when the claimant over-rotated, causing her legs to jack-knife towards her body as her body rebounded off the bed.

- A claim was made on the basis of incorrect teaching as the claimant was allegedly taught to 'flick her shoulders back' to rotate into the backdrop. The teacher denied this.

Judgment:

- The claim was upheld.

- The judge decided that the claimant believed she had to 'flick her shoulders back' to rotate into the backdrop even though, in all probability, the teacher had not taught the movement in this way. The claimant's perception of how the skill was to be performed caused over-rotation and injury.

Issues to consider:

- Great care should be taken when teaching technical skills.

- Progressive steps should be practised with reference to earlier learned practices when necessary.

- Pupil understanding should be checked at each stage of the correct and safe mechanics of any skill or part-skill.

Case 99

Activity: Trampolining
Age: Secondary
Principle: Clear communication and understanding between teachers and pupils

STAPLEY v ASHFORD BOROUGH COUNCIL
Queen's Bench Division, 1989
Transcript: Laidler Haswell
Lexis

Summary:

- This case came to court six years after the incident occurred.

- A 14-year-old girl was injured on the trampoline at a local leisure centre.

- The claimant alleged that she asked the instructor's permission to perform a somersault on the trampoline. He agreed and stood on the corner of the apparatus.

- The trampoline bed was more powerful than the claimant was used to and she over-rotated, injuring her arm as she put it out to protect her head.

- The claimant had some experience of trampolining and was a keen gymnast.

- The Borough Council accepted that the instructor should have stood closer to the performer at the time of the incident.

- The instructor argued that the claimant did not ask permission to perform the somersault so he had no reason to stand close.

- The claimant had attended trampolining at the centre before but not for approximately a year before the incident. She had been trampolining at school more recently.

- The claimant had warmed up on the trampoline and the incident happened during the third turn on the apparatus.

- Between 20 and 30 pupils were supervised by one instructor and were using three trampolines side-by-side.

- Another witness stated that the instructor was distracted by someone on another trampoline at the moment the incident occurred and that the claimant (her sister) had asked permission prior to performing the somersault but her recollection and evidence differed from that of the claimant.

Judgment:

- The judge accepted the statements of the claimant and other witnesses stating that permission had been sought and given, despite the variations in evidence. He also accepted that the instructor was 'entirely competent, careful and a good man...well qualified to do the job'. The judge found the girls to be reliable witnesses on the essential matters of the case.

- The instructor was judged not to have been standing where he should have been. It was not considered to be a deliberate disregard for someone's safety but he was still held to be at fault. 'He may have been over-persuaded...that she was very competent and did not require any particular instruction.'

Issues to consider:

- Effective communication between adults and performers is very important in order to be absolutely clear about what performers are to do during high-risk activity performances.

- Decisions should be based on observation and judgements on performance, rather than the possible persuasive nature of a performer.

- Up-to-date knowledge and practice in supporting is required. Such knowledge would have persuaded the responsible adult that he was not standing in the right place to provide appropriate support.

5.7 CASES RELATING TO HEALTH AND SAFETY

Case 100

Activity: Adventure activities
Age: Secondary
Principle: Gross criminal negligence – involuntary manslaughter

> **R v ELLIS**
> **Manchester Crown Court, 2003**
> **The** *Daily Telegraph* **and the** *Daily Mail*,
> **23 September 2003**

Summary:

- A boy drowned after being swept over the edge of a freezing 3 m-deep pool during an adventure activity organised by a school.

- His mother, a support worker at a secondary school, had asked if the 10-year-old boy could join the group of older pupils.

- The teacher in charge was experienced in leading outdoor adventure groups.

- The teacher ignored warnings that heavy rain had turned the stream into a torrent, which had swollen the plunge pool where the activity took place. Other groups had opted out of similar activities because of the conditions. The teacher was warned by staff members of the other groups that the conditions had become dangerous.

- The pupils participating in the activity lacked buoyancy aids, safety equipment, specialist clothing and ropes.

- The water temperature, at eight degrees Celsius, equalled that of the sea in February.

- The boy jumped in but panicked in the cold, swollen water. The teacher jumped in to help but was overcome by the cold temperature. The boy's mother and another pupil also jumped in but could not save the boy from being swept away.

Judgment:

- The teacher received a 12-month custodial sentence for manslaughter and a concurrent six-month sentence under Section 7 of the Health and Safety Act 1974, for failing to provide adequate care for the rest of the group.

- The judge saw video evidence of the state of the plunge pool that day and said, 'It was unbelievably foolhardy and negligent that anyone would venture into that beck when it was in such a state of spate'.

Issues to consider:

- Risk assessments should be carried out for all adventure activities. Contingency planning for an alternative programme should also be prepared, in case the environmental conditions on the day require this.

- Appropriate safety equipment should be readily available during all adventure activities.

- Advice from experienced personnel should be considered seriously.

- The wisdom of including younger pupils in an activity that has been planned to be challenging for older pupils must be questioned.

- The inclusion of family members in a party should be questioned. It may deflect the adult member of staff from professional duties.

Case 101

Activity: Adventure playgrounds
Age: Pre-school/primary
Principle: Failure to respond to Health and Safety Executive improvement notice

MOULEM v COUNCIL OF THE CITY OF CARLISLE
Queen's Bench Division, 1994
ELR
Lexis

Summary:

- A commercial operator of a play centre failed to take sufficient action upon receipt of six 'improvement notices' issued by the council under Section 4 of the Health and Safety at Work Act 1974.

- One of the improvement notices related to a rope bridge, which had deteriorated in condition and was a risk to those using it. The rope work was worn with frayed spliced joints.

- The improvement order was to remove and replace the existing rope bridge with one that was 'not worn, damaged or otherwise defective...and securely attached to the permanent structure'.

- Work had been carried out but what had been done fell far short of what was necessary.

- The commercial operator contended that Section 4 of the 1974 Act was intended to protect workers only and did not extend to the protection of lawful visitors to the play centre, including the children who used the equipment provided there.

Judgment:

- The appeal was dismissed.

- It was held that both Section 4 and the wording of the long title of the Act included the protection of those visiting the centre as well as those working there.

- It was further held that Section 3 (1) of the Act required an undertaking to protect the general public.

Analysis of Case Law to Identify Issues for School Staff, Coaches and Volunteers

Issues to consider:

- The plant, systems of work and procedures for health on site must be safe for both visitors and those working there. This is a responsibility of those controlling non-domestic premises (ie the governors, head teacher and school staff).

- Equipment, facilities and systems of work should be checked regularly. Defects should be reported and the appropriate action should be taken.

- Equipment, facilities or systems of work affected by an improvement notice must be replaced, repaired or adjusted to fully satisfy the order. They should not be used again until they have been approved.

- In *Webb v Rennie 1865*, Judge Cockburn, said that 'to continue to use defective equipment is prime facie evidence of neglect'.

Case 102

Activity: Canoeing
Age: Secondary
Principle: Inadequate safety systems

R v KITE
Court of Appeal, Criminal Division, 1996
2 Cr App R (S) 295

Summary:

- This is the case of the Lyme Bay canoeing tragedy.

- A managing director owned a company that organised leisure activities for young people.

- Four young people drowned while canoeing on the open sea.

- The company was accused of gross negligence as it failed to maintain proper safety standards and to provide sufficiently experienced leaders, which was deemed to be a substantial cause for the deaths of the students.

- Complaints from centre staff about safety had been logged with the centre a year prior to the incident but no action had been taken to remedy the inadequacies, which included no first aid kit and no towline.

- One of the accompanying teachers could not control his canoe and repeatedly capsized early in the journey. One of the instructors was very inexperienced. The group drifted out to sea and got into difficulties. The canoes became swamped, the students capsized and four students died.

- Standards were alleged to be woefully deficient.

- The managing director admitted to not knowing that inexperienced staff were employed.

Judgment:

- In the first instance, it was held that the manager was guilty of negligence but that there was no criminal intention. He had been unaware that students were undertaking trips of this kind.

- He was convicted of manslaughter for his failure to establish proper safety systems.

- At appeal, the custodial sentence was upheld but reduced from three to two years.

Issues to consider:

- When using activity centres, staff should check whether the centre is licensed under the Adventure Activities (Safety of Young Persons) Act 1995 and comply with the regulations arising from the Act.

- If licensing is not a requirement, it should be ensured that tutors' qualifications and levels of experience are adequate, that equipment is appropriate, and that risk management procedures have been implemented in order to provide proper safety systems.

- Pupils should not be taken, or allowed, into situations that are clearly beyond their level of competence.

Case 103

Activity: Horse riding
Age: Secondary
Principle: Failure to adhere to health and safety procedures

LEEDS CITY COUNCIL v THE PHOENIX EQUESTRIAN CENTRE
Leeds Crown Court, 2003
Daily Mail, **8 August 2003**

Summary:

- A 13-year-old girl died after falling from her horse when she fractured her skull on a concrete stable yard.

- She was riding without a saddle or bridle and had borrowed someone else's safety helmet, which was so big that it was loose on her head.

- The girl had been a pupil at the centre for four years.

- On the day of the incident, the girl groomed her horse after returning from an unsupervised ride. She then mounted the horse to take it back to the paddock, using a lead rope but riding without a saddle or bridle.

- As the girl took the lead rope, which was passed to her by another girl, the horse became excited, broke into a canter and threw the girl off on to her head.

- The centre owners were elsewhere in the office and other staff were taking their lunch breaks. The owners admitted to breaching the Health and Safety Act by failing to provide adequate supervision.

Judgment:

- The owners of the centre were given a conditional discharge. This was because the maximum level of penalty was limited to a fine and they had been declared bankrupt after losing their home and business. The judge said that there was no alternative to the conditional discharge.

- It was held that 'at no stage was there any proper supervision of the riding activities. If there had been proper supervision, it is clear the girl would have been prevented from carrying out the risky manoeuvre she did'.

Issues to consider:

- It is essential to have health and safety procedures in place and to ensure that they are adhered to at all times.

- Supervision that is adequate to the demands of the activity and the age, ability and experience of those involved is essential.

- Young people need to be involved in their own safety from the earliest ages so that they can recognise potentially hazardous situations and respond appropriately.

- Essential safety equipment should be used and no *short cuts* should be taken for convenience.

Case 104

Activity: Swimming
Age: Secondary
Principle: Inadequate supervision

A DROWNING CASE
NAHT Bulletin 51, 1995

It has not been possible to identify the case title and hearing information about this case, despite enquiries made to the Health and Safety Executive (HSE), the Royal Society for the Prevention of Accidents (RoSPA), the Amateur Swimming Association (ASA) and the National Association of Head Teachers (NAHT). The author has chosen to include the case details with the available information because of the importance of the principles involved.

Summary:

- The HSE prosecuted an independent school's trustees under Section 3 of the Health and Safety at Work Act.

- A 14-year-old boy died as a result of a *silent drowning* incident during a swimming lesson.

- The pool was 30 m by 10 m and the depth varied from 0.9 m to 2.1 m.

- The clarity of the water was good but roof glazing caused some reflection on the surface of the water.

- The teacher was well qualified.

- He was solely responsible for 40 boys in the pool and a further four non-participants. Some of the boys were new to him.

- The teacher verbally checked the boys' swimming abilities. They were then paired off. The better swimmers practised in the deep end. At the end of the lesson, those wishing to do so, swam the length of the pool in pairs – from the deep end to the shallow end.

- The boy who died was of limited swimming ability and had a limited command of English.

- The teacher may have been concentrating on another pair swimming slowly when the boy went under.

- At the end of the lesson, the class changed and the teacher claims to have checked the pool. The body was discovered half an hour after the lesson.

Judgment:

- The school's trustees were held liable.

- A fine of £21,000 was imposed. This equated, then, to a teacher's salary and reflected the extra supervision deemed to have been necessary.

- The judge referred to the ratio of pupils to teachers. In his opinion, the class required a ratio of one teacher to 20 pupils in line with existing guidance provided by the ASA.

- He also referred to the ASA/HSE *Safety in Swimming Pools* document, which describes the action required if reflection prevents swimmers from seeing the bottom of the pool clearly.

Issues to consider:

- Prior knowledge of pupils' dispositions and behaviour is important.

- The following guidelines are taken from the subsequent *Fatal Accident Enquiry 97:6 (95):*
  - Adequate levels of supervision are essential, taking into account prevailing circumstances and situations that may arise.
  - All staff need to be aware of the *silent drowning* phenomenon.
  - Head counts and scrutiny of the bottom of the pool should be regular.
  - If glare is affecting vision, those teaching should regularly move in order to be able to see all areas of the pool without glare. If this is not possible, they need to ask whether the class should be in the water.
  - The adult in charge should know the class and ensure effective communication with pupils who may have limited hearing, understanding or command of English.
  - There is a need for comprehensive, written, understood and applied operating procedures and emergency action plans.
  - The LEA/school policy and guidelines for safe practice should be followed.
  - Safe ratios, based on thorough risk assessments, should be determined.

5.8 CASES RELATING TO THE OFFENCES AGAINST THE PERSON ACT 1861: VIOLENCE IN SPORT

Case 105

Activity: Football
Age: Adult
Principle: Criminal assault – actual bodily harm

> **R v BIRKIN**
> **Court of Appeal, 1988**
> **10 Cr App R(S) 303, Crim LR 854**
> **Lexis**

Summary:

- During a game of football an opponent made a late tackle on the defendant without involving direct violence.

- Following the tackle, the defendant ran alongside the opponent before punching him. This was said to be a *spur-of-the-moment* act. He broke the claimant's jaw in two places.

- The defendant had several previous convictions for assault.

- There had been much verbal abuse between the two teams before the incident.

- The defendant regretted his actions but the judge deemed that 'he was disposed to the use of violence in the past' but in non-sporting circumstances.

- The defendant was charged for causing actual bodily harm contrary to the Offences Against the Person Act 1861.

Judgment:

- An eight-month prison sentence was imposed in the first instance, following a guilty plea.

- 'This court cannot repeat too strongly that incidents of this kind, on...the field, cannot be tolerated.'

- The prison sentence was reduced to six months at appeal.

Issues to consider:

- School staff are responsible for the acts of pupils participating in games, as the particular staff member responsible is the last adult to place the pupils in that situation.

- A single, *spur-of-the-moment, off-the-ball* outburst cannot be predicted but, when it happens, it is foreseeable that it may occur again. School staff/coaches should consider action in order to prevent repetition of the behaviour.

- Prior knowledge of a pupil's disposition and behaviour is important.

Case 106

Activity: Football
Age: Adult
Principle: Criminal liability – unlawful wounding

> **R v SHERVILL**
> **Court of Appeal, 1989**
> **11 Cr Ap R (S) 284**
> **Lexis**

Summary:

- A player was booked for dissent in a football match. He lost his temper and, in a subsequent struggle for the ball, kicked an opponent in the mouth while the opponent lay on the ground.

- It was an isolated incident in the match.

- The offending player was suspended by the league for two years and fined £100.

- He admitted to unlawful wounding.

Judgment:

- A six-month prison sentence was reduced to two months at appeal, as it was an isolated incident.

- In the first hearing, the judge said, 'Some people seem to think that if they commit acts of violence on a field of sport, they do not put themselves in the same position as those who commit acts of violence off the field of sport and elsewhere. That is not so'.

- Justice Tudor Davies also said, 'Any incident on a field of sport which involves foul play causing injury such as this is a serious matter'.

Issues to consider:

- School staff should insist that players, staff and parents accept the referee's decision without challenge.

- Team managers on the touchline should immediately substitute or remove from play anyone exhibiting violent conduct, either on or off the ball.

- Parents and other spectators verbally or physically abusing others should be asked to leave the premises. Incidents should also be reported to the head teacher.

Case 107

Activity: Football
Age: Adult
Principle: Criminal assault – actual bodily harm

R _v_ LINCOLN
Court of Appeal, 1990
Lexis

Summary:

- A player attempted to take a throw-in during a football match. An opponent stood immediately in front of the player and restricted his freedom to throw. This was within the rules. After the throw-in, as both players followed the ball, the player punched the opponent on the jaw, breaking it in two places.

- A linesman and the team manager witnessed the incident but neither thought the blow was of sufficient importance to warrant reporting the incident.

- No action was taken by the football authorities at that time but, subsequent to the initiation of legal action, the player was later banned for one year.

- Six weeks after the event (the claimant was off work for a total of eight weeks) the injured opponent reported the incident to the police. The accused denied knowledge of what had happened. He was considered to be a man of good character prior to the incident.

Judgment:

- The defendant was found guilty of assault occasioning actual bodily harm and was given four months' imprisonment, which was reduced to one month at appeal.

- Judge Boreham said:

  Only one blow was struck and that on the spur of the moment, and no doubt in the heat of the moment...which witnesses did not regard as a matter serious enough to report. However, justice required the imposition of an immediate custodial sentence...it was a serious matter. The provocation, if any, was very slight indeed. It is sufficient, to mark the gravity of the offence, and as a warning to others, to limit the sentence to one of 28 days' imprisonment.

Issues to consider:

- Pupils assaulting others should be immediately withdrawn from the game, if not sent off by the official, as it then becomes foreseeable that the event may occur again.

- Team managers have legal responsibilities for the behaviour of pupils, regarding the repetition of reckless or intentional acts outside the rules and spirit of the games.

- Staff should ensure that pupils understand, and play within, the rules and culture of the game.

Case 108

Activity: Football
Age: Adult
Principle: Criminal liability – grievous bodily harm

> **R v ROGERS**
> **Court of Appeal, 1993**
> **15 Cr. App R (S) 393**
> **Lexis**

Summary:

- A player fouled an opponent in a football match. Following the foul, he kicked the opponent and fell to the ground. As he got to his feet another player, who had not been involved in the incident, ran 10–20 m towards the opponent. He proceeded to launch himself with both feet off the ground and headbutted the fouling player, causing a displaced fracture of the cheekbone.

- The injured player was off work for four weeks.

- The accused expressed remorse and claimed a momentary loss of control in a highly charged game. He was deemed to be of previously good character.

Judgment:

- The defendant was found guilty of grievous bodily harm and was sentenced to nine months' imprisonment. This was reduced to four months at appeal.

- It was held that, when the opponent headbutted the other player, he committed 'a wholly unjustified and quite outrageous assault. There was no excuse for deliberate and dangerous behaviour'.

Issues to consider:

- Serious assaults on the sports field would almost always be punished with imprisonment if the police became involved. Minors may be liable to some form of detention and the responsible member of staff may be accused of secondary liability if it can be proven that they taught or encouraged the assault. There may also be secondary liability if the responsible adult failed to respond adequately, such as by immediately removing the player from the match on the grounds that it was then foreseeable that the player may repeat the unacceptable action.

- Team managers have legal responsibilities for the behaviour of pupils, regarding the repetition of reckless or intentional acts outside the rules and spirit of the games.

- The issues of fair play and sportsmanship should be emphasised.

Case 109

Activity: Rugby
Age: Secondary
Principle: Violent play – grievous bodily harm – secondary liability of the staff

---

R *v* CALTON
Court of Appeal, 1998
2Cr App Rep 64 CA
The *Daily Telegraph*, 29 September 1998

Summary:

- During a school rugby match, a 19-year-old student kicked an opponent so violently in the face that the impact 'sounded like a gunshot'.

- As the opponent got to his feet from a ruck the defendant kicked him on the side of the head, breaking his jaw in several places.

- The defendant admitted to grievous bodily harm.

Judgment:

- The student was given 12 months' detention in a young offenders institution.

- Justice Moore said, 'The injured boy was taken out after the ball had gone...any sportsman, boy or adult, who deliberately assaults another will face immediate custody to prevent others from doing the same'.

Issues to consider:

- The defendant's father is reported to have said:

    This is not justice. It was only a boys' game. Yes, he kicked and he admitted he kicked but this was a game which was rough from the start, all the players were involved in the spirit of the game. The supporters were all cheering on the players, adding to the fervour. What happened to my son is grossly unfair...it was in the heat of the game.

    It is worth considering whether the father's claim could be considered justifiable.

- School staff and coaches have a responsibility, as the last adult to place pupils on the pitch, to monitor rough, reckless play *off the ball* and/or beyond the laws and spirit of the game.

- Team managers have legal responsibilities for the behaviour of pupils, regarding the repetition of reckless or intentional acts outside the rules and spirit of games. Reckless play, and repetition of such behaviour, should be prevented by the responsible adult in charge. This may involve immediately removing the offender from play or even abandoning the game if, as a team manager, the official in charge does not take appropriate action because reckless play makes the possibility of injury outside the rules of the game foreseeable.

- The adult in charge should be pro-active when educating and enforcing the laws and spirit of the game.

Case 110

Activity: Rugby
Age: Adult
Principle: Criminal liability – grievous bodily harm

R _v_ GOODWIN
Court of Appeal, 1995
16 Cr. App R (S) 885
Lexis

Summary:

- A player deliberately struck an opponent with the point of his elbow after the opponent kicked the ball over the player's head and ran past him during a rugby league match.

- The blow resulted in a fractured cheekbone, jaw and palate, and damage to two teeth.

- The referee sent the player off the field. He was subsequently banned for 14 months.

- The player denied deliberate action. He had no previous history of violence.

Judgment:

- The defendant was imprisoned for six months for grievous bodily harm under Section 20 of the Offences Against the Person Act 1861.

- At appeal, it was held that a custodial sentence was not wrong in principle. However, it was reduced to four months because of the 14-month playing ban.

- Justice Mitchell said, 'This was a deliberate act of violence which, in my opinion, can be met with nothing other than a sentence of imprisonment...although he...behaved in the way he did on the _spur of the moment_ without intending to cause any really serious injury'. This decision distinguishes this case from _R v Lloyd 1989_ (Case 111, page 247).

- The judge also said:

  An important consideration...is whether the criminal violence occurred at or about the time one or other of the parties was playing the ball. Clearly, if the assault occurred then rather than when the ball was being played elsewhere on the field, it may be possible to take a less severe view of the offence. In such circumstances, if serious injury resulted the claim that the seriousness was unintentional and unexpected may be made with more justification.

Issues to consider:

- The infliction of injuries during play may be considered accidental, but injuries inflicted *off the ball* must be deemed deliberate and may be deemed criminal.

- Late tackles and acts of obstruction or violence away from the point of play must be dealt with severely. This may include sending the offender from the field of play, if the incident is deemed sufficiently violent to cause serious injury, or to have been performed with reckless intent.

- This judgment reinforces the policy of team managers on the touchline immediately substituting or removing from play anyone exhibiting violent conduct, on or off the ball.

Case 111

Activity: Rugby
Age: Adult
Principle: Criminal liability – unlawful wounding

R v LLOYD
Court of Appeal, 1989
11 Cr App R (S) 36
Lexis

Summary:

- A player was fairly tackled by his opposite number during a game of rugby union. The ball was released and rolled away from the tackle.

- The appellant, who was not involved in the tackle, ran up to the opponent and, without provocation, deliberately kicked him in the face, causing a fractured cheek bone.

- The appellant was of previously good character. He denied the offence.

- The referee did not see the incident.

Judgment:

- 18 months' imprisonment was imposed for grievous bodily harm with intent. This was upheld at appeal.

- Justice Pill said:

  Rugby union football is a game involving physical contact between players. Forceful contact is permitted by the rules. The game is not, however,...a licence for thuggery. In the course of the game, opportunity for thuggery may present itself. It is essential that players show self-control at all times and play within the spirit and letter of the rules. It is a sad thing when criminal law has to be invoked over an incident on a rugby field. What the appellant did had nothing to do with rugby football. It was a vicious and barbaric act...intended to cause really serious bodily harm.

Issues to consider:

- The fact that the appellant ran some distance to inflict the injury was deemed to prove intent. Should this be observed in a school match, the responsible adult should either shout to distract the offender from his intent or, if close enough, step in to prevent the battery. The player should then be immediately substituted and the incident fully analysed after the event.

5.9 CASES RELATING TO CHILD ABUSE IN SPORT

Case 112

Activity: Swimming
Age: Secondary
Principle: Child abuse

> **R v DREW**
> **Snaresbrook Crown Court, 2001**
> *The Times*, 30 June 2001

Summary:

- A former Olympic swimming coach systematically abused young teenage boys over a period of 25 years.

- The coach groomed the swimmers, making them believe that the sexual act would stimulate particular hormones and was beneficial to improving their swimming ability. The swimmers, anxious to become champions, believed the coach in whom they placed implicit faith as an adult and mentor.

- He convinced the young swimmers that he could help their swimming careers through medical means, which involved touching them and 'moving their hormones around their body'.

- The attacks took place in swimming pool changing rooms, hotels and at the coach's home.

Judgment:

- The coach was convicted and sentenced to eight years' imprisonment.

- He is to be placed on the sex offenders register when released as he is deemed to remain a risk to young boys.

- The judge said that the young swimmers had been in awe of the coach, who was crucial to the development of their careers. Their trust in him had been abused.

Issues to consider:

- It is important to recognise that physical, sexual and emotional abuse are closely related.

- All children have the right to protection from abuse.

- All suspicions of abuse should be taken seriously and responded to quickly and appropriately.

- Staff should learn to recognise the signs of abuse.

- Allegations of abuse are difficult to refute. Procedures should be established in order to avoid situations, whenever possible, in which a member of staff is alone with a pupil.

- Parents should be kept informed of supervisory arrangements.

- Procedures should be established regarding physical contact and support, which cannot be misconstrued.

- It should be ensured that the employer's requirements for disclosure certification are completed before anyone begins to work with pupils.

- It is important that staff liaise with the person in school who is responsible for child protection procedures.

Case Law in Physical Education and School Sport:
A Guide to Good Practice

LAW REPORT ABBREVIATIONS

Further case details may be obtained by researching transcripts in the following law reports. Details of the year the case was heard, the volume number and the report abbreviation are provided (where readily available) within each case heading in Chapter 5. For cases where this information was not readily available, the media source is provided. Cases that went unreported are cited without reference to a source.

AC	Appeal Court Reports
All ER	All England Weekly Reports
KB/QB	King's/Queen's Bench of the High Court Reports
LR	Law Reports from all courts
TLR	Times Law Reports
WLR	Weekly Law Reports
WR	Weekly Reporter

Other sources include:

Croner	*The Head's Legal Guide* and other Special Reports
Informa Professional Publications	Periodical journal *Sports Law, Administration and Practice*
NAHT	National Association of Head Teachers, *Bulletin 51*
National newspapers	*The Times/Daily Telegraph/Daily Mail – dates supplied*
O-Pro Group	*No Mouthguard No Defence,* First Edition 2001
Zurich Municipal Insurance Company	*Court Circular* periodical – dates supplied

GLOSSARY

Appeal
When proceedings move to a higher court in an attempt to overturn the judgment made by a lower court

Civil law
The law that addresses disagreements between individuals

Claimant
The person making the legal claim (previously known as the *plaintiff*)

Common law
The general principles that are based on judges' decisions and historical local customs that have become formalised over the years. These principles provide case law precedent for areas not covered by statute

County Court
The court that deals with minor civil claims

Criminal law
The law that addresses offences serious enough to be deemed offences against the state

Crown Court
The court that deals with serious criminal offences

Defendant
The person being sued (in civil cases). The person accused of the crime (in criminal cases)

Duty of care
The responsibility that everyone has to take reasonable care in any situation where harm to someone else could be foreseeable

High Court
The court that deals with serious civil claims

Higher duty of care
The standard of care expected with increased experience and specialist expertise. Through training or experience, one may be expected to visualise more clearly and anticipate more readily the results of one's actions in an area of specialism

In the first instance
Reference to the initial judgment made by a lower court (in cases that proceed to a higher court for appeal against the initial judgment)

Liability
The state of being liable (ie being held responsible for the loss or injury)

Magistrates' Court
The lowest form of criminal court that deals with all cases, either to reach a judgment or to send the case to a higher court

Negligence
The failure to fulfil a responsibility of duty of care, which results in damage, loss or injury

Regulations The Statutory Instruments, more commonly called Regulations, which provide the administrative detail for statute law. These set out the rules for how the law is to be applied and carry the force of law

Standard of care The level of competence associated with the proper discharge of professional duties

Standard of proof The level of proof that must be made evident for a judgment in favour of a particular party. In civil cases, this is based on *the balance of probability* (likely). In criminal cases, it is based on the higher level of *beyond reasonable doubt* (sure)

Statute The legislation created by Parliament in which rules of conduct for the protection of society remain in force until repealed. Statute law is binding on all courts and takes precedence over all other sources of law

Trap A hidden hazard

Vicarious liability The legal responsibility an individual, group or organisation (eg an employer) has for the actions of someone else

254

INDEX